# Children's York

## A guide for all the family

Bryan Waites

THE REDCLIFFE PRESS

*First published in 1981 by*
*Redcliffe Press Ltd.,*
*14 Dowry Square, Bristol 8*

For Gillian, Delia, Donna and Paul

Printed by Burleigh Ltd., Bristol
ISBN 0 905459 35 0

# Contents

*"Kirkgate", Victorian street reconstruction, with Hansom Cab in foreground.*
*Castle Museum.*
*(Photograph courtesy of Castle Museum)*

# About this book

York is magic. It brings the past to life before our very eyes and it makes your dreams come true. But it is not just a place, it is an experience. Whether you see it in the bleak mid-winter or in the busy, jostling summer it will captivate you. Never try to see York in a day for that is impossible. A lifetime is not enough. Plan your route. Think carefully where you want to go. This guide is designed to help you to do this. Allow yourself enough time to get the best from York.

If you are visiting try to avoid the busy summer months as you will find queues everywhere. This guide gives opening times and other details but remember that these may have changed. Check where possible. Beware of dangers near the river, from traffic on busy roads, in high places and elsewhere. Remember you are like a guest visiting a house and be courteous at all times.

For residents, we hope the guide will bring together useful information about York and encourage you to find out and join in many of the activities going on in this fine city. As residents you are entitled to free entry to many places and you have much more time to get to know and enjoy the unknown city.

Of course, we are grateful to so many people for their help in the compilation of this guide, both directly and indirectly. However, special thanks must go to the staff of the Tourist Information Office, the Central Library, the Curators of the Museums and the York Archaeological Trust who kindly answered queries. To the Chief Superintendent of the North Yorkshire Police and the Editors of the *Sports Directory* and other publications such as *Access* and *Living in York*. Grateful thanks also to Mrs. Jean Macfarlane for helping to discover the need for a guide like this, to Mrs. Ann Lambourne and other booksellers who received the idea with enthusiasm. To the Area Manager, British Rail Eastern Division, Rowntrees and other firms which kindly provided useful information and to Roger Thomas who drew several sketches. We shall be grateful to hear of any omissions, inaccuracies or additional information for future editions. All photographs, except where otherwise indicated, were provided by the Tourist Information Office – our thanks, again, to them.

**Bryan Waites**

**May 1981**

# Watching a city grow

IMAGINE you have a helicopter which can travel back through time. It is a Time Machine which will take you to any year in the past. You press the button and find yourself hovering above a plain in the north of England about fifty years before the birth of Jesus, *that is* 50 B.C. What can you see?

There is a small river flowing into a larger one. Marshland seems to be everywhere. The rivers have cut through a low ridge which is about eighty feet high. There are a few huts on the drier ground in clearings above the marsh. *This is Eburacon, the place where the yew trees grow and the Brigantes live.*

*It is three hundred and fifty years later, that is* A.D. 300. As you look down everything has changed. There is a large fort between the rivers. It is surrounded by a stone wall with watch towers at various places. Inside the fort there is much activity along the well-made roads and between the barracks and other fine buildings. Ships can be seen on both rivers and there are wharves also. A bridge links the fortress with a town on the other side of the larger river. In the town there are large villas with gardens and many streets. Outside the town cemeteries can be seen. *This is the Roman fort and town of Eboracum.*

*The time is five hundred years later, that is* A.D. 800. You can see that some streets and buildings are still there but many seem derelict. You can see where the fort used to be and ramparts have been built up with earth. There is one new stone tower. One large building in the fort is still used. Near it there is a large wooden church. Marshland and flooding can still be seen down near the rivers. Some activity is visible at the riverside and there are a few tiny wooden churches in the town. *This is the Saxon town of Eoforwic.*

*It is two hundred years later.* Below there is a large,

7

thriving town with many more streets and churches. The old Roman bank and wall has vanished in parts but some of it can still be seen. New defences, mainly of earth and palisades, have been placed on top of the old walls which have crumbled away. Defences can be seen down to the smaller river, the Foss. Beyond the larger river, the Ouse, there is also a settlement and a defensive rampart. In the centre of the town a Royal Palace can be seen, also a large church. There are many ships and merchants at the riverside and between the rivers south of the Palace many thatched workshops and houses can be seen. *This is the Viking town of Jorvik.*

*It is only one hundred years later, that is* A.D. 1100, but there are many changes. There are two castles on mounds. The defences have been improved and for extra defence there are moats around the castles and walls. The River Foss has been allowed to flood as a natural defence and for use as a fishpond. There are many streets and churches. There is a large Minster Church where the Roman fort used to be. Outside the walls the Abbey of St. Mary's is being built. There are many houses beyond the Ouse and the Foss. *This is the Norman town of York.*

*The year is* A.D. 1300. Fine stone walls with great gateways surround all parts of the large town. The Castle between the rivers is much larger. There are only two bridges. Many streets wind around like a maze inside the walls. There are also streets outside and some follow the line of the walls. There are signs of industry and trade on and near the rivers, with wharves and many boats arriving up river from the North Sea. There are many fine timber and stone houses. You can see monasteries and so many churches that you can hardly count them all. In the centre, where once the Roman fort stood, is a huge Minster but it is only partly completed and you can see the masons at work on the nave. *This is Medieval York.*

*Carved stone figures in the Minster.*

*Now your helicopter has taken you on to the year* A.D. 1800. The city walls are largely in a ruined condition. The Castle doesn't look so much like a castle now as it has been turned into a prison and court house. Its buildings look very fine and, in other parts of the city, there are similar splendid buildings such as the Mayor's Mansion

9

House, the Assembly Rooms where great balls took place. Although there are no new churches you can see the Theatre Royal and many large coaching inns such as the Black Swan. Eight roads lead to the city and they are well maintained. The daily stage-coaches are on the way to London. Inside and outside the city the roads are crowded. Many markets can be seen in the centre. A New Walk has been laid out along the river and at Knavesmire there is a racecourse. Micklegate and some other streets are full of new, impressive houses. Some people have moved out of the city to build fine houses in the suburbs. As you look closer you can see slums within the walls. Above all towers the majestic Minster. *This is Georgian York.*

*The Year is* A.D. 1880. A very great city lies below you. The city walls have been restored in many places and work is going on to restore other sections of wall. In one place an arch has been made through the wall to allow railway trains to enter and reach the station in Toft Green. But outside the wall a large and impressive new Railway Station and Hotel has just been completed. The city is the centre of railway networks. There are new bridges across the rivers at Lendal, Skeldergate and Scarborough Railway Bridge. In the city there are many new buildings such as the Art Gallery, Law Courts, banks, shops and offices. Within the walls in Walmgate there are terraced houses for workers. Factories can be seen. Some areas are slums. The city is spreading far outside its walls now. There are terraced houses, schools, colleges, churches and chapels far and wide. The Minster sits serene marking the place where York was born one thousand eight hundred years before. *This is Victorian York.*

*Now your helicopter brings you back to today* and you can take out your map to see the York of the twentieth century. Surrounding villages have grown to join in a continuous sprawl of houses. Often they follow roads now busy with cars, lorries and buses so that places like

10

Fulford and Acomb are linked to the city with houses all the way. The railways are even more noticeable. Large factories like Rowntree's, Craven's and Terry's lie beyond the walls. Trade and shipping seem to have vanished from the rivers though pleasure boats can be seen. Hospitals, new schools and a university are visible together with a large waterfront hotel. A great outer by-pass road runs round the city several miles away. Though this takes much traffic there is still congestion in the narrow city streets. The Minster seems better than ever as it presides over nearly two thousand years of history. Many other now famous buildings and streets appear cleaner and more attractive. Everywhere people seem to be looking around as tourists and they come and go between car and coach parks. At night we can see the city lit up with some of its famous buildings floodlit. *This is our York, twentieth century York.*

York has evolved over two thousand years into the great city it is today. Layer upon layer of history have been added. If we walk round today we can find clues to tell us about this past. Archaeologists each day dig into the ground to discover even more about York. Yet in many ways, despite change, the city remains the same. There are still the two rivers meeting together near the castle; still the unique walls and the eternal Minster. They are the fixed features in a changing city. Now more than 100,000 people live in York and each year over *two million* tourists visit. York has become more than a place in the north of England—it is the city of our dreams and it belongs to the world.

Two books will tell you more about York's story: *A Town Grows Up* by Ursula Aylmer, Oxford Children's Reference Library no. 16 and *2000 Years of York—The Archaeological Story*, The York Archaeological Trust, 47 Aldwark, York YO1 2BX.

You should start your visit to York by going to St. Mary's Heritage Centre, Castlegate, where you can hear and see the *York Story.*

11

# Visiting the Heritage Centre

HAVE YOU heard about the church that was sold for 5p? It was St. Mary's, Castlegate, within sight of Clifford's Tower. In 1958 St. Mary's, like so many other churches in our city centres, was closed. Most of its congregation had left the city to live in the pleasant suburbs.

What could be done with this beautiful but redundant church? Should it become a warehouse or super-market as many chapels and churches have become? If possible it is better to find a more appropriate use as a museum or youth centre.

The City Council had an even better idea. Why not use St. Mary's to tell the *York Story*—how the city grew during two thousand years? With this in mind they bought the church for 5p in 1972 and by 1975 it opened. That was a good year to open as it was European Architectural Heritage Year when all over Britain and Europe people reminded themselves how lucky they were to have so many fine historic buildings. They realised that such buildings should be looked after or *conserved* before they were lost forever.

Inside, St. Mary's has been skilfully converted. As you enter there are colourful panels showing the Growth of York. Then you pass The Scaffold which shows men at work as though they were actually building the church in medieval times. The central part of the church is about Medieval York and there are models of the Shambles, the riverside, brilliant shields and many other murals. Look for the trick item in the riverside diorama—can you find the deliberate mistake?

There are models of King's Manor and St. William's College and an attractive display on the Merchant

12

Adventurers' Hall. Look for the Execution scenes, the Siege of York and the Battle of Marston Moor. The Burlington Room commemorates Lord Burlington who brought the new Italian style of architecture into Yorkshire. He designed the Assembly Rooms and did great work elsewhere with his friend William Kent, a Bridlington man. The Room contains a figure of the young Lord and has panelled walls, a gilt mirror and a gambling table reflecting the rise of York to become the social and pleasure capital of the North in the 1700's.

Further on John Carr, York's famous architect, is remembered in a display of his life and works. Outside St. Mary's you can see Fairfax House (1756) and Castlegate House (1762) which he designed. Nearby, the buildings close to Castle Museum (The Female Prison and the Assize Courts) were by Carr in 1773/80 (see *Famous People* chapter).

As you pass along up the stairs can you find 'Efrard, Grim and Aese'? Soon you will see the large model of the City with displays about planning problems. Go into the theatre for the slide, music and commentary on York. Before leaving go into the South Chapel to see the rare stained glass. Can you find the spider? Look for the display on York & The Railway.

Various publications are on sale in the Heritage Centre.

*Opening times:* Weekdays 10.00 a.m. to 5.00 p.m. Sundays 1.00 p.m. to 5.00 p.m.

*Admission charges:* Cheaper between November 1st and March 31st. Joint ticket available for the Castle Museum and Heritage Centre but this is only advantageous during summer months.

All enquiries to the Curator, Castle Museum (tel. 53611).

*A Roman soldier of the Ninth Legion.*

14

# Roman York

THE FAMOUS Ninth Legion marched from Lincoln in A.D. 71. When they reached the land of the Brigantes they chose a site for their fort between the Rivers Ouse and Foss. No one knows yet whether or not the Brigantes already had a settlement there.

At first the fort and its ramparts were made of wood and earth, a little like the U.S. Army forts in the Wild West. Eventually, these defences were replaced by strong stone walls and towers with impressive gateways and main streets. The military headquarters was called the *Principia* and it was sited where the Minster is now. Around it were barracks, stables and baths. There were two main streets—the *Via Praetoria*, now beneath Stonegate, and the *Via Principalis*, now beneath Petergate.

The Via Praetoria led to a bridge over the Ouse and into the civilian town called a *Colonia*. This bridge has disappeared but it was located between the present Guildhall and Riverside Gardens. Both rivers would be busy with trade and it is thought that the Roman dock area was along the Foss.

The Ninth Legion, a body of more than 5,000 men, had been stationed at York for about forty years when, suddenly it seems, they were replaced by the Sixth Legion. Historians thought that the Ninth marched out of York one day to quell rebels further north and that they were annihilated in a nameless, unknown battle. Such was the disgrace that the Romans never mentioned the Ninth again.

This is a nice idea for patriotic Britons to keep but recent research is showing another story—a far less interesting story. Now it is believed that the Ninth was transferred overseas to Nijmegen, then later to Palestine where it was destroyed in battle about A.D. 161.

Because York was a Roman town for almost three

15

hundred and fifty years we can find many signs of it in the present-day townscape, even though later building has hidden so much. *Let's go on a tour to discover Eboracum.*

Start in the *Yorkshire Museum* and the *Hospitium* in the *Museum Gardens.* These contain one of the finest collections of Roman objects in Britain including tombs, coffins, coins, inscriptions, everyday items and jewellery. You can find out how the Romans lived and died. There is a statue of Mars the God of War which was found in Blossom Street in 1880. Look for the Mosaic of Four Seasons in the Museum.

*Opening times:* see page 21-22.

*Admission charges* to the Museum but the Hospitium and Museum Gardens are free.

Still in the Museum Gardens look for the *Multangular Tower.* This was at the west corner of the Roman fortress. There is a stretch of wall and remains of another tower adjoining. If you go through a little door into the garden of the Public Library you can see behind the Tower and wall. Here you will find a display to explain the construction. You can see how the Saxons, Danes and Normans built into and on top of the Roman wall. There are Roman coffins on' the lawn nearby and, under an arch near to the main gates of Museum Gardens, you can find more Roman remains.

As you leave the Museum Gardens and pass into Museum Street look opposite. Another interval tower has been excavated at the corner of Lendal Street and Museum Street but this will eventually be displayed in the basement of the building being erected on the site.

Go to *Bootham Bar* and you may see on your left a plaque on a section of wall built in A.D. 300. Bootham Bar sits over the site of one of the Roman gateways and as you look down Petergate think that once this marked the line of a main Roman road.

16

You can walk round the city walls from Bootham Bar to *Monk Bar*. As you do, remember that this wall was built on top of the old Roman wall. You turn a right-angled bend on the wall which marked the north corner of the fortress.

If you carry on a little beyond Monk Bar you will see the remains of two towers, one, the *Aldwark Tower* marked the eastern corner of the fortress. You look down on them from the present wall.

Now go to the *Minster* and visit the *Undercroft* where you can see the remains of the Roman HQ, the Principia, plus other finds from recent excavations (see page 45 for opening times).

As you leave the Minster by the south door look for the Roman column nearby. This was found *under* the Minster in 1969 and re-erected here.

Finally, go down *Stonegate*, which as you remember was also one of the main streets in Roman times.

Excavations will continue to reveal Eboracum to us. Most of it still lies beneath our feet. In 1972, for example, a fine Roman sewer was discovered under Swinegate. As you look around beware of the ghost of the legionaire—he has been seen!

You will find these books useful and interesting:—
*Roman York from A.D. 71: A Pictorial Guide* by H. Ramm.

*Eboracum* by Peter Wenham.

There is a storybook called *Eagle of the Ninth* but if you want the latest research read *The Fate of the Ninth Legion* by E. B. Birley in *Soldier and Civilian in Roman Yorkshire* (ed. R. M. Butler).

*The Roman Army* by Graham Webster.

# Finding the Vikings in York

HAVE you seen York's biggest hole in the ground? It was dug near Coppergate between 1976 and 1980. At its deepest it was over thirty feet and it was at least as large as an Olympic swimming pool. It was in this hole that you could find most of Viking York.

Of course, you may be too late to see the hole now for it was due to be filled in during 1981. On top of it a large shopping precinct will be built.

This hole is an archaeological excavation begun by the York Archaeological Trust in 1976. Layer upon layer has been stripped away until, in the deepest layers, the Vikings have been discovered. It is like opening a window to see their life one thousand years ago.

The Vikings raided Northumbria and captured York in the year 866. Ten years later, in 876, Halfdan became the first Viking King of Northumbria and he chose York as his capital city. The Vikings called it *Jorvik*. For almost eighty years the city was ruled by Viking Kings but in 954 King Eadred of Wessex drove out Erik Bloodaxe, the last of the Viking Kings. In their place he left an Earl to rule for him. These earls ruled Jorvik until 1066 when William the Conqueror arrived.

But Jorvik still remained a mixture between Viking and English. It is true to say that for two hundred years between 866 and 1066 Jorvik was the second largest and second richest city in all Britain with many connections with Scandinavia. Most of its people still thought of themselves as Vikings.

Can we look through the Coppergate window to see how they lived? More than 10,000 finds from the hole

18

in the ground will answer this question. The water-logged soil near the River Foss has preserved many finds in excellent condition just as though they were made yesterday.

The timbers of buildings have been uncovered which were workshops as well as houses. Coppergate means the street of the woodworkers and it seems from the finds that this was one of the activities carried on there.

The buildings followed the same directions as later shops and houses on the site. Many seemed to have a narrow frontage onto the street then extending a long way back. As well as woodworkers there were metal-workers, carvers of bone and antler, workers in bronze, amber and glass, leather workers producing shoes and boots. Silver pennies were made there, clothes, pottery, gold and silver ornaments—even chessmen made from Whitby jet.

Wooden whistles and pan-pipes have been dis-covered, a lady's silk headscarf, knives, axes, pins, brooches, buckles, beads, belts, bags, combs and ice skates made from bone (used on the frozen Ouse). It is even possible to find out the diet of the Vikings with oysters coming out as a popular dish!

It is clear to see that Jorvik was a rich centre of trade. The Viking Royal Palace is believed to have been where King's Square is now. From it streets or 'gatas' led to the Minster (Monkgate), to the river ford (Ousegate), to the wharves (Fossgate), and to the south (Micklegate). Outside the walled defences were the fishermen (Fishergate) and a little further away outlying villages called 'thorpes' were found, now known by names such as Layerthorpe and Copman-thorpe.

As you can see, Viking York was much bigger than our hole in the ground but we need many more holes in the ground to really recapture it all as it was. When the chance comes again to excavate in the city more will be revealed about Vikings and other peoples. A chance

*(i) Viking footwear from Coppergate from left to right: an adult's ankle boot, a child's ankle boot and a child's shoe.*

*(ii) The Director of the Coppergate Site trying out the unique set of wooden pan pipes, which are still playable after 1,000 years.*
*(Photographs courtesy of York Archaeological Trust)*

to excavate the waterfront alongside the Foss in 1981 had to be given up because money was short. This would have shown us what the Roman and Viking docks were like. Now, if buildings are put on the site the chance will have gone for ever. Archaeologists are always racing against time and money (see *Dig This* chapter).

## Where to find the Vikings today

*Coppergate:* You may still be in time! You can see the site, visit the display including slide show, replica Viking boat, etc., and the shop with its interesting items such as Hnefatafl—the Viking War Game, replicas of finds at Coppergate including pendants, brooches, armrings, etc.
*Opening times:* Daily 9.00 a.m. to 5.00 p.m.
*Admission charge.*
Enquiries to York Archaeological Trust, 47 Aldwark (tel. 32342).

When the new shopping precinct is completed, there will be a Jorvik Viking Centre below it which will tell the story of the Viking capital. A great exhibition of the Coppergate finds is planned to open in York Spring, 1982.

*The Yorkshire Museum* has Viking finds on display. The coin collection can be inspected by prior arrangement (tel. 29745/6).
*Opening times:* Monday–Saturday 10.00 a.m. to 5.00 p.m. Sunday 1.00 p.m. to 5.00 p.m. Open Good Friday.
*Admission charges*, but a family ticket is available.

*The Hospitium* is in the grounds of the Yorkshire Museum and contains Viking finds.
*Opening times:* Easter to the end of September. Monday–

21

Saturday 10.00 a.m. to 5.00 p.m. Sunday 1.00 p.m. to 5.00 p.m.
*Admission free.*
Free admission to both for school parties making advanced application.

*York Minster Undercroft* has a small display of Viking-age gravestones (see *York Minster* chapter for opening times, etc.).

*St. Mary's Church, Bishophill Junior* has the only visible standing building from Viking times in York. It is part of the tower. So far nothing has been found of a Viking cathedral which many think existed. There are some Viking remains in St. Mary, Castlegate (The Heritage Centre), All Saints, Pavement, and Holy Redeemer, Boroughbridge Road.

*Lloyd's Bank, Pavement* has a small display about Viking finds excavated on the site in 1972.
*Opening times:* Normal banking hours.

*The Anglian Tower* in Museum Gardens shows a cross-section through the defences including Viking additions.
*Opening times:* Monday–Friday 7.30 a.m. to dusk.
    Saturday 8.00 a.m. to dusk. Sunday 10.00 a.m. to dusk.
*Admission free.*

When you have visited these places and seen many of the wonderful objects they made and found out about their way of life you will know that the Vikings were not the savages, heathens and barbarians that so many people thought them to be.
*Jorvik Viking Age York* by R. A. Hall will tell you more (from York Archaeological Trust and local shops).

# The view to do

YORK is very flat and the best places for a view of the city are from the walls, from the Central Tower of the Minster and from Clifford's Tower.

Clifford's Tower is almost like the leaning Tower of Pisa—it looks as if it will collapse any minute. It seems to lean outwards on top of its mound and if you look closely you will see large cracks in it. Yet it has been here since 1245. Actually, the mound or *motte* was made in the time of William the Conqueror. He built a wooden castle on it and, below the motte, he had an enclosure called a *bailey* surrounded by a bank and ditch. In the bailey was a hall, chapel, barracks, stables, kitchens and workshops. He dammed the River Foss to provide a moat round the castle.

Go up the fifty-five stairs leading to the entrance. Look at the Royal Coat of Arms and the Clifford Arms above the door. Which is which? Can you see the holes and slots of the old portcullis? As you pay to go in ask for the booklet about Clifford's Tower on sale at the kiosk; also buy the rolled sketch of *York in the XVth century*. Both are quite cheap.

Now, as you enter the keep you must imagine when it had floors and rooms. Look for the well and fire-places. Climb the stairs and walk around the top but be very careful!

Perhaps you have noticed that it isn't round. In fact, the Tower is shaped like four circles interlocking with each other. This is called a *quatrefoil*. There is no other building in England like it.

If the wind isn't too strong you can open up your sketch. This tries to show what York may have looked like about five hundred years ago. Look towards the Minster and, using the sketch, pick out the various landmarks, such as the walls, rivers, Ouse Bridge, etc. How much has it changed?

23

*A view of the leaning Clifford's Tower with Dick Turpin's sign in the foreground.*

Now go round the Tower so that you have a view south. You are looking down on Castle Green—that's the oval in front of you. It's called the 'Eye of Yorkshire'. From 1801 until 1868 it was the site of the gallows. People were hung in front of a crowd there.

The fine buildings around the 'Eye' are now the Castle Museum and the Assize Courts but as you will see from your sketch this was once the lower part of York Castle. Look to your right across the River Ouse and you will see another mound. This is *Baile Hill*, the site of William's second castle to control the river but it did not last very long and now there is little but the motte to see. To your left was the *King's Pool* caused by the damming of the Foss. This was drained in 1853 and built over.

It's a wonder Clifford's Tower is still intact for it developed a huge crack in it in 1358, it was bombarded during the Siege of 1644 and burnt out in 1684.

Besides, the ghosts of 150 Jews massacred there in 1190 may still haunt the site.

By the way, did you see St. Mary's Heritage Centre? That's the lovely spire on the Minster side of the Tower. If you missed it go round to look for it.

*Opening times:* May–September 9.30 a.m. to 7.00 p.m. daily.

October, March, April 9.30 a.m. to 5.30 p.m. weekdays. 2.00 p.m. to 5.30 p.m. Sundays (April 9.30 a.m. to 5.30 p.m.).

November–February 9.30 a.m. to 4.00 p.m. weekdays. 2.00 p.m. to 4.00 p.m. Sundays.

Closed for lunch 1.00 p.m. to 2.00 p.m. October–March.

Closed Christmas Eve.

*Admission charge:* Parties of schoolchildren admitted free but give ten days' notice to Department of the Environment, Crown Buildings, Duncombe Place, York. Season tickets available also.

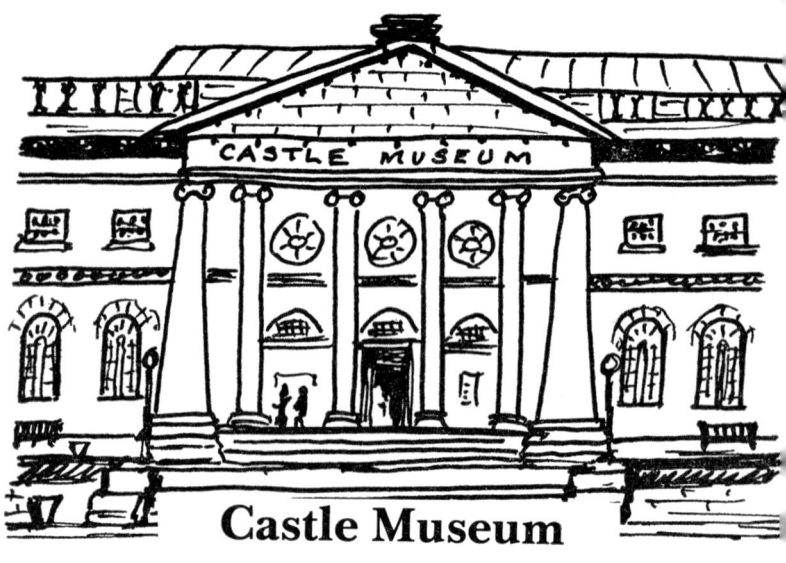

# Castle Museum

DR. JOHN KIRK visited his country patients through-out the North Yorkshire Moors for many years. As he did so he used to collect all sorts of things, from fire-places and furniture to toys and farming tools. People thought it was strange to bother with all this junk but Dr. Kirk realised that one day such items would be scarce. In fact, people would not know about them at all or even recognise them. They came from a time, nearly one hundred years ago, which most of us cannot remember. Now we call such items 'bygones'.

His collection grew so large that he had to find a better place to store it and to show it. In 1935 the City of York agreed to convert part of York Castle into a museum. On St. George's Day, 1938, the Museum opened. There had never been a Museum like this one before for it brought the past to life. Since that time it has expanded into the largest and most popular folk museum in Britain.

What makes it so different? Go into the wonderland inside and you will see. There are *Period Rooms* which take us into a *Victorian Parlour* of the 1870's (can you find out what a painted purdonium, an aspidistra and an antimacassar are?); a *Moorland Cottage* (see the peat fire, the patchwork quilt and the crystoleums(?)); a *Georgian Room* of the 1720's (look for the Grandfather Clock and Willow-pattern pottery); and a *Dining Room* of the 1690's (what is a bridewain?).

Then there is the *Yorkshire Gallery*, *The Green Gallery* (with 250 truncheons, Whitby jet ornaments and Valentines from 1797 onwards) and the *Chapel Gallery* (with country life and farming the main theme). Look for the huge collection of fire insurance plates and the many lovely scale models of ships, etc. Can you discover the meaning of cow-ties, kits, back-cans, strickle, havercake and clapbread?

Visit the *Music Gallery* to find the oldest virginal plucked by quills—what on earth is that? See the history of fireplaces in the *Hearth Gallery* and go into the *Dales Farm*—can you see 'Pat the Giant'?

But the best of all is to walk down *Kirkgate*, a real street from the past with grocers shops, silversmiths, pawnshop, spirit store, butchers, apothecary's, toys, tallow chandlers and many more. All the shop fronts were collected and rebuilt here. Look for the Sheriff of York's State Coach, the stage coach, the fire station, the Hansom Cab. The shop windows contain lots of things you will have never seen before. Can you find Phineas and the plate with Dr. Kirk, Surgeon, on it? Look for Quintilian, the pot dog to the right of the pawnbroker's window. In a story he has the power to bring all the other toys to life. Every Christmas, carols are sung in Kirkgate and it comes to life even more than usual.

Walk from Kirkgate into *Princess Mary Court* and see Joseph Terry's sweet shop, the padded cell and Thomas Cooke's shop. Can you find Minerva? You will find the *Military Collection* super with its medals, decorations, armour and uniforms of Yorkshire regiments and don't forget to see the largest collection of costumes in the

27

country nearby. There are also many, many toys including one of the oldest dolls houses in the world, games and talking dolls.

Finally, *Half Moon Court* will take you back to Edwardian times and the former cells of the prison have been converted to workshops which you can peep into. Here you can see the work of a comb maker, a clogger and a pipemaker as well as many others.

Eventually you will come to 'Pompey's Parlour', the Condemned Cell where Dick Turpin was prisoner in 1739. Outside you can visit *Raindale Mill*, brought stone by stone from the North York Moors and rebuilt on the site of the old castle mill. Look for the remains of the old castle wall nearby. When the Mill is open you can see it working and buy stoneground flour in canvas bags.

*Opening times:* April–September weekdays 9.30 a.m. to 6.00 p.m. Sundays 10.00 a.m. to 6.00 p.m.
October–March weekdays 9.30 a.m. to 4.30 p.m. Sundays 10.00 a.m. to 4.30 p.m.

*Raindale Mill:* April–September only 9.30 a.m. (10.00 a.m. Sunday) to 5.00 p.m.

*Castle Museum* is closed Christmas Day, Boxing Day, New Year's Day, but open Good Friday (tel. 53611).

*Admission charge:* Cheaper between November 1st–March 31st. Party rates available during this period only.

During May, June and July, school parties are admitted only by advanced application. Enquiries to the Curator tel. 33932 (afternoons only).

Joint ticket available for Museum and Heritage Centre.

Half an hour after closing allowed for visitors already in the Museum to finish looking around.

*The Museum Shop* has a guide, booklets and souvenirs on sale. There are useful Castle Museum Walks available.

*(i) Go window-shopping down a Victorian street – inside the Castle Museum.*

*(ii) Witness a scene in the trenches of World War I, reconstructed in the Castle Museum's Military Gallery.*
*(Photograph courtesy of the Castle Museum)*

29

*One of the best ways to see York: walking along the City Walls.*

# Round the Walls

ONE of the best ways to see York is to do the Wall Walk. The length is about three miles and it will take you about two hours. It is a safe route, mostly away from traffic, and you get excellent views of the city from different angles. You can leave the wall to look into the city at many places and then return to it later to continue your trail. The walls are the longest and finest in Britain and they look lovely in Spring when the banks below are covered with daffodils. As we have seen (see *Roman York*, etc.), they are built on top of the defences made by earlier peoples for the most part. It is the medieval wall built during the thirteenth century that we can walk along today. However, we couldn't walk very far along it if it had not been for the restoration of one hundred years ago. This turned the ruinous walls into the marvellous sight we see today by adding walkways, arches, battlements and some towers. Even now the restoration and upkeep of the walls carries on.

Before we go very far along the walls we must learn their language. Here are some of the code words:

Bar means gateway as in Monk Bar.

Barbican . . . defensive parallel walls linked by an

arch which stick out in front of a gateway as at Walmgate Bar.

Bartizan . . . an overhanging turret as on Bootham Bar.

Battlements . . . the lower and higher parts of the wall which make it like a fort. You can peep through the lower parts which are called embrasures.

Buttress . . . a stone or brick pillar which supports a wall.

Parapet . . . a low wall on the edge of a roof, tower, bridge, etc., to protect against the sudden drop.

Plinth . . . the projecting base of a wall.

Portcullis . . . a gate which can be pulled up and down usually found in castle gateways.

Postern . . . a small gateway.

Rampart . . . stone wall or wall of earth surrounding a castle, fortress or fortified city.

Turret . . . a very small tower often round and attached to another tower or building.

Now, armed with these wall words you can attack!

**The Best Wall Walk** (for those in a hurry)

Start at Bootham Bar. This gate stands on the site of the north-west gate of the Roman fortress and is still the road to Scotland. Look for the bartizans, the statues on top of the Bar, carved in 1894 to replace older ones, the coats-of-arms of the Stuarts and the City. Can you see remains of the portcullis?

As you walk along the wall you follow the line of the Roman fortress walls. Look towards the Minster and its beautiful Dean's Park. This is one of the most attractive views in York. You will see glimpses of the Minster Library and the Treasurer's House (see *Famous Buildings*). Carry on to Monk Bar. Before you reach it there is a depression in the ramparts which marks a Roman gateway, now long gone. If you look down towards Chapter House Street you can see how a Roman road once led to this gate.

Monk Bar is one of the best gateways but you cannot go through it. Go down to the street then up to the wall again. The portcullis is still in working order. Look for the shields and the statues of the six wild men ready to drop stones on the enemy's head.

If you wish you can now go to the Minster down Goodramgate or carry on to Layerthorpe Postern along the wall. If you carry on you will see to your right Roman fortress remains and the Merchant Taylors' Hall (see *Famous Buildings*). You arrive at the Postern, where the wall ends because the River Foss and the King's Pool provided a water defence.

## Things to see for those with time for the complete Wall Walk

*Red Tower.* From Layerthorpe Postern to Red Tower there is no wall. A great lake was enough, but now it has gone. Red Tower was built in 1490 and caused a battle because stonemasons resented the bricklayers building it. Look for the projecting lavatory.

*Walmgate Bar.* The only gate to keep its barbican, portcullis and wooden gates. Enemies had to attack by entering the barbican which was very dangerous. Look for the Elizabethan House fastened to the back of Walmgate Bar.

*Fishergate Bar and Postern.* You will eventually come to both. Keep looking back towards the Minster. Can you see the two medieval inscriptions on the Bar? Note the new Swimming Pool on your left. It is on the site of the Cattle Market (1827–1970). You are now near the Foss. From the Postern there used to be a chain hung across the river. Why? You could step down from the wall a while to visit Dick Turpin's grave in nearby St. George's Churchyard (see *Famous People*). Once the Foss was much wider here.

*York Castle.* This was the main part of the walled defences (see Castle Museum and Clifford's Tower). You will have to visit on another occasion if you want to keep going round the wall. Cross Castle Mills Bridge looking for Raindale Mill. Then over Skeldergate Bridge to join the wall at *Baile Hill*. This is William the Conqueror's other castle mound of 1068.

*Micklegate Bar*. The most important gateway from the south. Kings and Queens came through it. Traitors' heads were hung on it. Look for Roman coffins used in building the lower part, little figures, the bartizans and shields.

You will walk round past the old railway station on your right and on your left you will see the present railway station. As you approach the river you will have one of the finest views in Europe looking towards the Minster but beware the traffic below you as the walls have few railings here. If time allows step off the walls to find the cholera burial ground in Station Road, a reminder of a deadly epidemic in the city in 1832.

As you cross over Lendal Bridge you might step into Museum Gardens to see the Roman wall, tower and the famous Anglian Tower. St. Mary's Abbey had its own walls and towers (see *Roman York* and *Monasteries and Mystery Plays*). Soon you return to Bootham Bar.

Did you notice the many kinds of arrow slits on your wall walk? There are at least twenty-five types. There are also different types of tower shapes as well as plinths.

A useful book is *The Bars and Walls of York* ·by R. M. Butler.

*Opening times:* The City Walls are open daily dawn to dusk, except in icy or snowy weather.

*Admission free.*

# Along the river

WHICH Yorkshire river has no beginning or end? The answer, the Yorkshire Ouse. A few miles north-west of York the River Ure changes its name to the Ouse then follows its winding course through York for 57 miles reaching the River Humber where it disappears just as easily as it appeared. Yet it is Yorkshire's most important river for it is joined by the Nidd, Wharfe, Foss, Derwent, Aire and Don—rivers which drain most of the north of England.

As we have seen, the Romans built their fortress between the Ouse and the Foss and as York grew from this site both rivers played an important part in its history. Since the Ouse was tidal ships could reach it from the sea. Viking invaders sailed up the Ouse to raid and plunder then later they settled. Their town of Jorvik became a great centre of trade. (See *Finding the Vikings in York*.)

William the Conqueror dammed the Foss to make moats for his castles, to give power to his mills and to provide fish. In the Middle Ages York was a great port especially in the wool trade. Wool and fine cloth were exported to many parts of Europe. Many other trades such as goldsmiths, silversmiths and saddlers flourished. Traders formed themselves into Guilds, rather like Trade Unions. One of the most important was the *Merchant Adventurers* who in 1357 built their splendid hall in Fossgate which you can still visit (see *Famous Buildings*).

York's prosperity came to an end by the eighteenth century. Trade went elsewhere as the rivers silted up, larger ships could not come so far inland, roads improved and York became a coaching centre rather than a port. Eventually the railways replaced the rivers as the main means of transport. The opening of Naburn Lock in 1757 and the canalisation of the Foss in 1793 improved things a little and cocoa beans together with some other goods continued to come up river.

Now the rivers are mainly used for water supply and pleasure. The Ouse supplies York with over ten million gallons of water a day.

There are lots of things to do on or beside the river—walking, fishing, rowing, sailing, pleasure trips on launches and even water skiing downstream at Cawood. Let's find some of the best places for walking first.

If you are at the Railway Station or the National Railway Museum you can cross the river on the pedestrian path over the Scarborough Railway Bridge. This avoids the busy streets and gives you a reminder how lucky it was for York that the modern railway is on the edge of the city rather than going through the middle. The bridge was built of cast iron in 1845. When you reach the east bank of the Ouse if you have time there is a pleasant walk upstream to Clifton, a mile away. Frequent buses will return you to the city.

If you turn right towards Lendal Bridge in the city you will have a pleasant riverside walk which has been fairly recently laid out. It passes the walls of St. Mary's Abbey and the Museum Gardens—a lovely place for a picnic.

*Hill's Boatyard* at Lendal Bridge, was founded in 1840. You can take a six-mile round trip on the Ouse taking about one hour. It goes as far as the Archbishop of York's thirteenth-century *Bishopthorpe Palace*. Daily sailings from mid-March to September in covered launches with a commentary. Parties should make prior arrangements on booking forms (tel. 23752). Rowing boats can also be hired here. Nearby is the *York City Rowing Club*.

Cross Lendal Bridge built in 1863 to the *North Street Postern Tower*. Here you can see steps to the ferry landing which operated before the bridge was built. Go down the steps and under the bridge into *Riverside Gardens*. This is another good place to rest and eat. Opposite is the *Guildhall* (see *Famous Buildings*).

Look into *All Saints Church*, North Street. Its slender spire is a landmark. Inside the church is really medieval in appearance and it has world famous stained glass windows. Walk alongside the river in front of the *Viking Hotel* to *Ouse Bridge*. About here the Vikings made their landings. Now the 10-storey, 100-bedroomed hotel towers 109 feet above the river.

Ouse Bridge was the only bridge across the river for centuries. Micklegate became the main road of York. In fact it was part of the high road from London to Scotland. At each end of the bridge down on the waterfront are the historic dock areas of York known as *King's Staith* and *Queen's Staith*. Can you see the old slogan 'Use the Ouse' on a warehouse? Does it look as though there is much trade on the river now?

The *King's Arms* is a very old inn. Can you see the flood marks on the walls? The river was always liable to flood during its long history. Walk further down the riverside along *South Esplanade*. Hill's launches operate from here also *Ouse Cruises* (tel. 32530) with day and evening trips daily in season and by arrangement out of season. These are sightseeing tours of the city as seen from the river. Another cruise operator with trips to Bishopthorpe Palace and the Ship Inn, Acaster, is *White Rose Cruisers* (tel. 704594) Wednesdays 3.00 p.m. to 9.00 p.m. only.

A little further downstream you will come to *St. George's Gardens*, another good picnic place with

*Clifford's Tower*, the *Castle Museum* and *St. Mary's Heritage Centre* close by. Notice the old wall which comes down to the river and the cottage sitting on top of the remains of *Davy Tower* on the edge of the Gardens. Can you find the wall plaque describing floods here? Opposite, across the river look for the *Old Customs Warehouse*.

Your walk can continue under *Skeldergate Bridge* built in 1881 into *St. George's Field*. This is now a big car and coach park but it is still the site of fairs and you may find one in full swing there at Easter, Whitsuntide, August and November. Again you can sit by the riverside for a picnic. This area is between the Ouse and the Foss. If you want to carry on further walk across the attractive *Blue Bridge* to Fulford Ings. You can get a bus back from Fulford Road. You will be near the site of the great battle of 1066.

The River Foss is not so easy to walk along as, in the city, it has either buildings or factories next to it. However, you can get a good view of *Raindale Mill* just below Castle Museum, from Castle Mills Bridge over the Foss.

Every summer there are regattas held by City and University Rowing Clubs. The *Yorkshire Ouse Sailing Club* is at Naburn five miles downstream. There is dinghy racing every weekend from March to October. The public are welcomed to watch but boats are not normally available for hire. The *York Motor Boat Club* is located at Fulford, in fact just a little way beyond Blue Bridge opposite *Terry's Chocolate Factory*.

If anyone wants instruction in *water skiing* this can be arranged by prior appointment at *White Cross Power Boat and Ski Club*, Cawood (tel. Cawood 216) but this is 13 miles south of York.

*One of the old warehouses to be seen along the river.*

*Pleasure craft lined up on the River Ouse, outside the imposing Guildhall.*

For the quieter pursuit of fishing, licences are available for Yorkshire Water Authority and York Amalgamation of Fishing Clubs' Waters from *Hookes of York Ltd.*, 28–30 Coppergate (tel. 55073) and *G. E. Hill*, 40 Clarence Street (tel. 24581). There is a good variety of coarse fishing in the York rivers. *The Northern Anglers' Handbook* will be helpful and you can get further information about Yorkshire rivers from the Yorkshire Water Authority, West Riding House, 67 Albion Street, Leeds LS1 5AA (tel. Leeds 448201).

*Riverside York* by Ivan Broadhead is a very useful leaflet available in shops and the official guide has a section on York's Rivers. Several walks in the *Bartholomew City Guide to York* follow the river and they are very fully described.

**Take great care at all times and in all places along the river. It can be very dangerous.**

# The heart of Yorkshire

WHEREVER you go in York you will see the Minster. It is the heart and soul of the city, in fact, there is a window in the Minster called the 'Heart of Yorkshire'.

The Minster stands where the Roman fortress was and there have been at least three previous churches before this one on the site, the first dating from A.D. 627.

The present Minster took 252 years to build being completed in 1472. It is the largest medieval church in England—524 feet long and 249 feet wide with the Central Tower 234 feet high. Like most churches it is built in the shape of a cross.

In 1407 part of the Central Tower fell down and it was discovered in 1967 that the foundations were so weak that it was in danger of falling again. An immense amount of money was collected and the foundations of the Tower and other parts of the Minster were renewed by 1972. That was a good year to make the Minster safe as it was the five hundredth anniversary of its completion.

It would be impossible to tell you the whole story of the Minster here or even to point out the many magnificent sights in it. You will find many books and leaflets to help you when you arrive. First there is *A walk round the Minster* which is freely available inside and includes small plans showing the location of interesting features. In the *Cathedral Shop* you will find *Let's Explore York Minster* and *Let's find out about the Minster* as well as a sheet of four *Minster Walks*. All these are quite cheap.

The *York Official Guide* has an excellent section on the Minster and there is much more in *Bartholomew City Guides: York* and *The Buildings of England: Yorkshire, York and the East Riding* by Nicholas Pevsner. The great

41

work is *A History of York Minster* by G. E. Aylmer and R. Cant.

There are many other souvenirs, gifts, slide sets, etc., in the fascinating Minster Shop. Also you can obtain information sheets from the Tourist Department at De Grey Rooms, on *Stonework* and *Woodwork in York* which include a great deal on the Minster.

Go quietly into the Nave of this great church and sit down. The sight could take your breath away and if you happen to be there during a service or when the organ is playing you will be even more impressed. Make certain to go beneath the Central Tower—the Lantern Tower as it is called—look up.

On your walk around see if you can find the 'Heart of Yorkshire', the Five Sisters and the Rose Window. The Minster and the parish churches of York contain the largest collection of medieval stained glass in Britain. The Great East Window is the size of a tennis court and is one of the largest and most important windows in the world. Can you find the oldest glass in the Minster dating from about 1150?

Keep your eyes open for tombs, tablets and monuments around the walls. Can you find the only Royal Tomb? Where is the Archbishop's Throne? York Minster is the only cathedral in England with its own police force. Can you find evidence of this? Look for Ulf's Horn. Who was he and what did he do?

See the Astronomical Clock and Gog and Magog striking out the time elsewhere. Look for the Kings of England carved on the Choir Screen—who do they start and finish with? Can you find angels playing different musical instruments? Did you see the mouse in the Lady Chapel?

Visit the largest *Chapter House* in Britain. It is octagonal—how many sides is that? How on earth is it supported? You have to look outside for the huge buttresses to discover how it stays up. The little carvings

on the seats around are interesting. Can you find out
what goes on in a Chapter House?

You can go down to look at the foundations of the
Minster and to find out about the Roman buildings on
this site. Make for the *Undercroft Museum*. The entrance
is near the shop and the South Door. You will see the
layer upon layer of earlier history beneath the Minster.

*(i) Exhibits in the Minster Treasury in the Undercroft include this Crusader's Casket.*

*(ii) Gargoyles on the Minster – don't be put off, it's well worth going inside!*

*The Treasury*, nearby, houses the precious possessions of the Minster.

At the eastern end of the Minster is the *Crypt*. You can ask a guide to take you into it. There you can see the Doomstone, altars dedicated to three famous saints and a font marking the site of the first wooden Minster of 627. Look also for the base of the Roman pillar.

Before you leave you should ascend the *Central Tower* for a view over the city. You need to be fit and to stand a few hair-raising episodes but it will be worthwhile. From the top you can see the pattern of streets and how the two rivers come together at Clifford's Tower. Notice how varied the roofs are, though pantiles seem everywhere. Look into the distance to see the Pennines and the Yorkshire Wolds. Can you see the power stations towards Ferrybridge and Drax?

Don't forget that the outside of the Minster is also worth a walk round. You could do with binoculars here to see the detailed carving high up. It is particularly pleasant in Dean's Park. If you are nearby at Noon you will hear Big Peter. He is 135 years old and has the deepest tone of any bell in Europe. He is also the third largest bell in England. Can you guess the two larger ones, in London?

At night, the Minster is floodlit and it still acts as the main landmark in the city almost like a torch pointing the way to Heaven.

*Opening times:* Daily from 7.30 a.m. to dusk. Details of
services, concerts, etc., posted on notice boards.

*Admission free* but there is a charge for the following:—
*Chapter House:* Open weekdays from 10.00 a.m. Sundays from 1.00 p.m.
*Central Tower:* Open weekdays from 10.00 a.m. Sundays from 1.00 p.m. No reduced price for children.
*Undercroft:* Open weekdays from 10.00 a.m. Sundays from 1.00 p.m. (tel. 54134).

There are reduced rates for parties. Guided tours, worksheets and various publications are available through the Information Officer, St. William's College, College Street (tel. 24426).

A great cathedral needs constant care and repair. You can buy a Minute of History whilst you are there if you wish and get a certificate for it. Also you can become a Friend of York Minster and help to make it safe and beautiful for all time.

# Monasteries and
# Mystery Plays

DO you remember that in the Robin Hood stories it was always the Abbot of St. Mary's, York, who was the rich priest getting himself captured most of the time? This great Abbey, founded in the 1080's, was one of the richest and most splendid in the whole of England. In size it must have rivalled the nearby Minster, for the church alone was about 360 feet long and there were also many monastic buildings attached.

You can see the ruins in the Museum Gardens (see page 21-22 for opening times, etc.). They are close to the Yorkshire Museum. Although the Abbey was outside the city walls it had its own defences which you can still see. There is the fine gatehouse near St. Olave's Church and towers at various places along the wall. If you look closely you may find masons' marks. Go into Marygate, which is a fine street, and walk down to the river. Here you will see St. Mary's Water Tower.

Back in the Museum Gardens the Hospitium was the Abbey guest house. Most of the remains of the monastery are in the Yorkshire Museum where you can see parts of the cloisters, the warming house and other sculptures, as well as a fragment of the shrine of St. William (see *Famous People*).

The Abbot's House is now known as the King's Manor (see *More Famous Buildings*) and though it has been extended it would always be a fine building. You can reach this via a small footpath from Museum Gardens behind the Museum.

Before you leave the Gardens look for the ruins of St. Leonard's Hospital, another religious house, which did a great deal of good for the people of York .in medieval times. Besides these houses, York had two

47

*Medieval ruins of St. Mary's Abbey.*

priories, four friaries, a nunnery and about fifty parish churches so you can see how important religion was in medieval York.

By the way, whilst you are in Museum Gardens look for the famous peacocks. The Gardens were specially laid out in the 1830's when the Museum was built and they contain a fine collection of trees and shrubs. A leaflet is available giving a plan and identifying the specimens (*Living Sculpture*, a guide to the trees in the Yorkshire Museum Botanical Gardens). You may also notice an odd-shaped building in the centre of the

48

lawns. This is the old *Observatory of York* built in 1832 and once essential for giving the correct time before the days of the radio 'pips'. A great effort is being made to save and restore the Observatory to its former glory.

## Mystery Plays

York had many Guilds in medieval times. These were usually groups of people following the same trade such as butchers and carpenters. There was a strong religious background to them. There are still some guilds in York even today. The craft guilds, each year, wrote and performed plays based on stories from the Bible. The plays date from 1340 and there are 48 of them. Each guild had its own play and its own wagon on which the play was acted. In June, the wagons assembled on Toft Green then they toured through the city stopping at a dozen places to act their play. The first stopping place was Holy Trinity Church, Micklegate. If you waited here all day you would see all the plays in turn.

You can still see the York Mystery Plays. They are still proclaimed by a herald on horseback, but except for one or two plays, they are not taken around the streets. Now they are performed, mainly by York citizens, every three years outdoors in Museum Gardens in front of the ruins of St. Mary's. The plays have been modernised and are played almost every night for three weeks as part of the *York Arts Festival*.

The next performances of the Mystery Plays are expected to be in June and July, 1983. For further details contact Tourist Information Centre, De Grey House, Exhibition Square, York YO1 2HB (tel. 21756). A very useful book which gives details of the route in medieval times is *The York Mystery Plays* by Elizabeth Brunskill.

49

## York's Guilds

Annual Service of the Company of Merchant Adventurers in All Saints, Pavement, on the Sunday nearest to January 30th (the day on which Charles I was beheaded in 1649).

Annual Service of the Guild of York Freemen in All Saints' also in April when they process from St. William's College.

The Lord Mayor and Corporation attend the Civic Service at St. Helen's Church in October.

Council Meetings are held in the Guildhall (see *More Famous Buildings*) about every four weeks when the Lord Mayor and Corporation attend in State. The public can attend. You can visit the Merchant Taylors' Hall, Aldwark, and the Merchant Adventurers' Hall, Fossgate.

*The forces of Good and Evil in conflict in a Mystery Play: Jesus (right), Lucifer and the masked Beelzebub.*

50

# Church quiz

ONCE, five hundred years ago, there were at least fifty parish churches within the walls of York. Now there are nineteen. Some of these are disused or turned over to community centres, arts centres or stores. Most have reduced congregations as so many people have left the city centre to live elsewhere.

Wherever you are in York you will be near a church. Look inside if you can as each one has a treasure of some kind for you to discover. Perhaps if you have seen the main attractions or if it's raining and you have nowhere else to go you can visit a church. If you do, here is a quiz to solve. Some of the questions can be answered from this guide as well as from going to some of the churches mentioned.

1.  Which parish church is world famous for its stained glass window showing the last 15 days of the world?
    All Saints, North Street *or* All Saints, Pavement.

2.  Which church has an octagonal lantern tower once a landmark to guide people through the marsh and forest?
    All Saints, Pavement *or* Holy Trinity, Goodramgate?

3.  Where is there a thirteenth-century door knocker showing the Devil swallowing a woman?
    St. Cuthbert, Peasholme *or* All Saints, Pavement?

4.  What was the first stop of the Mystery Plays where there are also stocks in the churchyard?
    Holy Trinity, Micklegate *or* Holy Trinity, Goodramgate?

5.  Which is the oldest parish church in York and the place where General Wolfe's parents worshipped?
    St. Denys, Walmgate *or* St. Cuthbert, Peasholme?

6.  Which was the church of the Guild of Glass Painters?

St. Margaret, Walmgate *or* St. Helen, Stonegate?
7. Which disused church is now York Arts Centre?
   St. John, Micklegate *or* St. Mary, Bishophill?
8. Which church was gutted in an air raid in 1942 but is now looked over by the Little Admiral and Father Time?
   St. Martin-cum-Gregory, Micklegate *or* St. Martin-le-Grand, Coney Street?
9. Where is a curfew tolled at 8 p.m. daily?
   St. Michael, Spurriergate *or* St. Olave, Marygate?
10. Which is the only church with Saxon windows and a Saxon Cross?
    St. Mary, Bishophill *or* St. Sampson, Church Street?
11. Where is the York Story to be seen and heard?
    St. Mary, Castlegate *or* St. Mary, Bishophill?
12. Where was Guy Fawkes baptised?
    St. Michael-le-Belfry, Petergate *or* St. Andrew, St. Andrewgate?
13. What church has a rest for a man's wooden leg in one of the pews?
    St. Olave, Marygate *or* St. John, Micklegate?
14. Which church has a squint, box pews and a rare saddle-back roof?
    Holy Trinity, Goodramgate *or* St. Margaret, Walmgate.
15. Which church roof was used as a gun emplacement during the Civil War?
    St. Olave, Marygate *or* Holy Redeemer, Borough-bridge Road?

Good luck on your church crawl! You will find an information sheet issued by the Tourist Department, De Grey Rooms, very useful. It is called *The Ancient Churches of York* and it has sketches of most of the churches mentioned above as well as brief notes. Best of all it's only 1p!

# Dig this

THERE are usually several archaeological excavations in York at any one time. The Coppergate dig may finish in 1981. Others, like Bedern and Walmgate, will have closed or be about to close. However, the York Archaeological Trust, set up in 1972 to carry out rescue operations on threatened sites, will have moved to new digs.

One of these is on the Castle Garage site opposite Clifford's Tower where a large hotel is to be built. The Trust hope to find evidence of Romans, Vikings and a Franciscan Friary here. Another city site may be in Coney Street where plans for new shops will allow excavation of the riverside areas. Outside the City Walls, near Monkgate, a proposed new hotel and leisure complex may be built over Roman houses and a medieval burial ground. If so, excavation would be valuable here.

The Trust has excavated as many as twenty sites since 1972 and kept an eye on one hundred and twenty-five other sites where they could not excavate.

Anyone interested in finding out more about active digs and possible visits to them should contact the York Archaeological Trust, 47 Aldwark, York YO1 2BX (tel. 32342). The Trust has a conservation laboratory, a pottery research centre, a drawing and editorial office, a finds store at St. Saviour's church and, in association with University of York, an environmental archaeology unit.

You can become a Friend of the York Archaeological Trust for a membership fee: Family £7.50, Children and Students £3.00. This will allow you free entry to Trust sites open to the public and regular organised site tours; attendance at lectures and on excursions; provide special social events and other activities. You will also

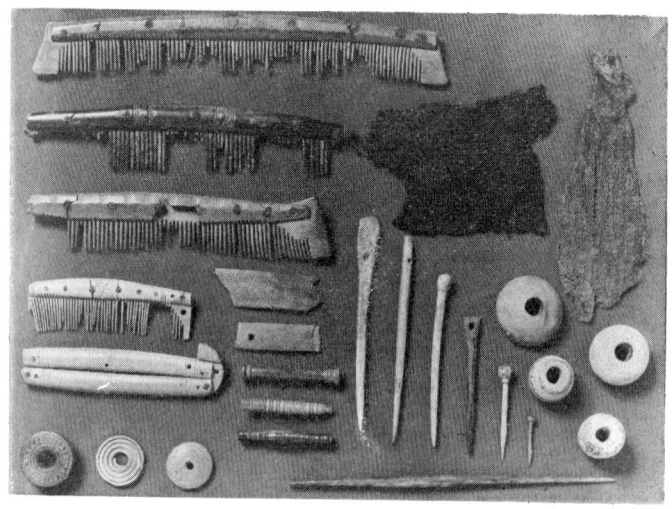

*10th century antler combs, York mint coin and ingot mould, spindle whorls for spinning and textile samples.*
*(Photograph courtesy of the York Archaeological Trust)*

get a free copy of the excellent *Interim* magazine which explains more about the digs in York. Write to the address already given above.

Because of insurance reasons people under 16 may not actually work on the sites but they can help in many other ways such as finds processing, etc. Local schools have helped in this way on a regular basis.

The Trust has a Schools Service which offers talks in schools linked to a later site visit. These are particularly for young people aged 8 to 18 years. The Schools Officer is willing to travel to any part of the country to give the talk with slides and display (where day return tickets are available). Schools staying in York can arrange a similar talk at their hostel but must provide a projector. A guided tour of a site can also be arranged to follow the talk. The present cost of this service is: Talk in school and guided site visit—60p per pupil plus travelling expenses: Guided site visit only—30p per pupil, adults 35p.

The Trust explains about the work of an archae- ological unit: where to dig, how to organise a dig, what to look for on a site, what you expect to find, what happens to the finds. Write to the Schools Officer, YAT, 47 Aldwark, York, for application forms well in advance (tel. 53991). Details of Young Rescue from here too—there is a local branch. Young Rescue is part of Rescue, The British Archaeological Trust. Members receive a lapel badge, membership card and four issues of the Newsletter each year. Ages 9 to 16, annual subscription £2.00. Activities, holidays, digs, competitions, lectures, etc. Enquiries also to Dr. Kate Pretty, New Hall, Cambridge CB3 0DF.

For details of gifts, publications and other items produced by the YAT write to the address given (Mail Order Department). A brochure entitled *Gifts from Viking York* is available. There are detailed reports on many of the digs.

# Some York loos

THIS list is in addition to the loos to be found in museums and public buildings:—
    *Bootham Bar (7.45 a.m. to 10.00 p.m. daily)
    *Minster Coach Park, Clarence Street
    Monk Bar Car Park
    *Museum Gardens, Museum Street
    Nunnery Lane Car Park
    Ouse Bridge (liable to flood!)
    *Paragon Street Coach Park
    Parliament Street (boys only)
    *Railway Station (main entrance 7.00 a.m. to 9.45 p.m. daily)
    *Rougier Street (West Yorkshire Bus Station 8.00 a.m. to 10.00 p.m. daily)
    St. Deny's Road, Piccadilly (permanently open)
    *St. George's Field (permanently open)
    St. Sampson's Square (girls only)
*Facilities for the disabled also.

*The Shambles by night.*

# Streets and shopwindows

MANY of York's queer-sounding street names are Viking in origin—Coppergate was the street of the woodworkers; Skeldergate, the shield makers street; Spurriergate, the spurmakers street; Goodramgate, said to be named after the Danish chieftain Guthrum; Swinegate, the swine market; Colliergate, the street of the charcoal burners and Micklegate, the great street. Other names came later such as Coney Street, the King's street; Ogleforth, owls ford; Pavement, the first paved street in York; Shambles, *fleshammels*—the street of butchers; Jewbury, the burial ground of the Jewish people who lived in the city. The meaning of York's shortest and queerest street, Whip-ma-Whop-ma-Gate is still not certain, some saying that it was the site where criminals were whipped, others that it just means the lane in between—so short that it hardly deserved a name.

Whatever the name you will find the streets of York one of the main attractions whether in the busy, bustling summer when you are almost knocked off the pavements by tourists or in the quiet of cold winter when you may have a street to yourself. One of the best times to be in York is just before Christmas when, as night falls, York turns into a real-life Christmas card before your eyes.

Even if you have only a few hours in York you can still get around many of the famous streets. A good place to start is from the Nunnery Lane car park. Here you reach Micklegate Bar in a few minutes to follow your shopping trail.

**Micklegate**

This long and marvellous street curves past Georgian

57

houses down to Ouse Bridge. If you use the *Miniguide* and/or the *Index Plan of York*, both obtainable from the Tourist Department, De Grey Rooms, then you will see this clearly. The *Historic York Pictorial Map* which you can buy at the same place will give you more information about the buildings en route.

There are two good bookshops which have interesting children's sections: *Ken Spelman* and the *Blake Head Bookshop*. The former is mainly secondhand with some good bargains. Opposite is a *Newsagents* at 85 Micklegate selling lots of paperbacks and guidebooks.

Don't forget to peep into the *Priory Street Sports and Community Centre* just off Micklegate where there are lots of activities going on and a cafeteria. *Neptune's Fish and Chip Shop* is at the corner of this street.

Further down Micklegate you will see *Saks Hairdressing Salon* which has a children's night and the *York Stamp Exchange*. If you are interested in this hobby you will want to go to *Stonegate Coins*, 16 Stonegate and *York Coin & Stamp Centre*, 4 Church Lane, later.

As you reach the bottom of the hill and come close to Ouse Bridge you pass the *Arts Centre* on your left. Near to *Boyes Store* you will see a riverside walkway which leads to Lendal Bridge. Cross over Ouse Bridge and look both upstream and downstream for good views. Just to the left on the other side of the bridge you will see *Songs & Stories* managed by Anne Lambourne which has lots of interesting things for children in the shop. *King's Staith* is down steps on the far side of the road and, nearby there is a *Wimpey* in Low Ousegate.

## Coney Street

Just turn the corner and there you are, in one of York's busiest shopping streets with *W. H. Smith's* excellent bookshop and many departmental stores such

58

*Petergate by day, with the Minster in the background.*

as *Leak & Thorp* and *British Home Stores. St. Martin's Rooms* often serve tea, coffee, soup, squash and light refreshments in the remains of the old church buildings. Look for the *Little Admiral* on the clock nearby. You can catch up on local news in the offices of the *Yorkshire Evening Press* which have copies of recent papers for you to look at, as well as posters of local events.

Coney Street runs into St. Helen's Square with the

59

*Mansion House* and *Guildhall* to your left (see *More Famous Buildings*). The *GPO* is just down Lendal.

## Stonegate

One of the finest streets anywhere. On the corner you will find one of Britain's leading music shops, *Banks & Co.* To go inside here is a real experience for it must contain just about everything in the music world: Action songs for schools, large study scores, harmony and theory books, band and wind music, recorder music, school song books, drill and dance, percussion and string music, Christmas music galore, guitars and guitar music—each floor is a musical galaxy!

Then there is *Pennyfarthing* which has posters, candles in a tin, cards, bank note pads looking like real money, little pennyfarthing bikes made out of real pennies and a bigger-sized version out back!

Look for *Mulberry Hall* and find the date. Can you see the *Stonegate Devil* at No. 33? *Kilvington's* is a fine shop for all your pet requirements. Bookshops, as always in York, are never far away. *Thomas Godfrey's* will keep you occupied for hours, expecially in the children's bookshop a little distance from the main bookshop. You will find the *S.P.C.K. Bookshop* interesting too. Do you know what the initials mean?

There are several interesting alleys off Stonegate. One of them, next to Pennyfarthing, leads to a new shopping precinct. Go into it to look at *Romany Toys*. They have ugly plastic faces which have revolving eyeballs and moving mouths as well as lots of other toys. This is an attractive precinct which has a glass roof giving good views of the nearby Minster.

Another alley is Coffee Yard leading to Grape Lane. Here you can reach *Upstairs and Downstairs*, a cafe with take-away burgers, pizzas, chips and ice cream.

Further on Stonegate changes its name to *Minster Gates*, a short street but full of interest. On the corner you can look up to see *Minerva* just above *York Insignia*.

60

Once there was a bookshop here and Minerva was placed above as the Goddess of Wisdom. Go into York Insignia to see the badges, crests, shields, books, ties, flags, t-shirts and many other items. You can ask if you have a crest and they will find out from a big book and tell you what it is. Then, if you can afford it, you can have it made into a shield to hang up at home.

Minster Gates also includes *Edwin Story's Book and Gift Shop*, especially good on local books. Also *E. & P. Barker's Toyshop* with exciting model trains including the original Rocket, steam wagons, an Advanced Passenger Train Set, and many more treasures. Close by is the *Potter's Wheel* and a secondhand bookshop called *Discovery Fine Art Books*.

## Petergate

There is a High and Low Petergate. Go into High Petergate first which runs in the direction of Bootham Bar. You will find *Minster Gallery* and *Memories of York*, interesting shops to look in. The former has, among other items, 100 different water colours (many of local scenes) by the artist Douglas Heald which make a striking display in the window.

Next down into Low Petergate, you will find *George Gadsby's* shop with artists materials and, lower down the street the amazing toyshop with the right name— *Precious*. This is a cavern of delight, especially at Christmas time when it bursts at the seams with people. Look for the moving puppet show, miniature train sets and also larger ones, dolls and everything you can think of in the toy world.

*Harding's Bookshop* is in this street, again an excellent place to browse. Across the way is the antiquarian bookshop of *McDowell & Stern*.

## Goodramgate

Running up to Monk Bar and full of unusual buildings and surprising side streets. Look for the oldest row of cottages in York, the fourteenth-century *Lady Row*. Slip into *Holy Trinity* down the passage nearby. About halfway up the street you will find a clutch of interesting shops: *Craftsmen* (lovely Paddington Bears, a village shop and other toys), the *Gift Centre*, *Libracraft*, the *Tigga Cafe & Restaurant Shop* and *Feelgood* where you can buy any number of badges from a selection of 100 each at 10p. Across the road is the *National Trust Shop*.

If you go right along to Monk Bar you will discover, almost hidden away under its arches, the *Monk Bar Model Shop* which is huge inside and small outside. Wonderful working models of all kinds, in the window at present a meccano moon vehicle making a successful landing. Opposite, is the *Monk's Bar Newsagency*, owned by Mrs. Butterworth, a very pleasant and well-stocked shop.

*Exotic Birds and Pets* is at 19 Goodramgate which reminds us of the other York pet shops—*Allpets*, 269 Melrosegate, *Mawson & Son* in Walmgate and *Acomb Pets* some distance out of the city at 13 Regent Buildings, York Road, Acomb (tel. 798963).

**Off St. Sampson's Square**

*Galt's Toyshop* is in the perfect setting down Finkle Street and is essential for a visit. Round the corner in Davygate is *York Model Centre* and in Newgate, amongst the bustling market stalls, is *Alpha Nova*, another treasure house where you can find wooden jig-saws, orange cookies, pottery money boxes, miniatures, wooden brooches and papier maché figures from Mexico.

**The Shambles**

Like walking into the Middle Ages. The marvel of York. A must for everyone. See *Derwent Crafts*, the *Giftshops*, *Woodcarvers of the Shambles*, *Belt Up*, *Design*, *Cox Sheepskins*, *Pickering's* fantastic bookshop and all the other sights. There is still at least one butcher in the street of butchers! End up in Whip-ma-Whop-ma-Gate to photograph the sign. Now a quick rush to nearby Colliergate to visit *Impressions Gallery of Photography* which has exhibitions, books, etc., you can join and use the darkroom, etc. Just before you prepare to go down into Fossgate you will notice a Wimpeys if you feel like a snack.

**Fossgate and Walmgate**

By now you will be getting tired but never fear! The end of your shopping trail is in sight. Did you have time to go into York's widest street, Parliament Street where you would see, among many other things, *Marks & Spencers*? Now you are on your way down to the River Foss. Look in at the excellent *Barbican Bookshop* which is full of nooks and crannies. You can't miss the splendid crest of the Merchant Adventurers which is over the passage leading to the Hall. Then take in the fine view to Clifford's Tower from the Foss Bridge. Don't forget access to the Barbican can be made through the bookshop. Further down into Walmgate you will come to the *Community Bookshop* at No. 73 which you will enjoy for the badges, posters and funny cards if not for the books. But maybe you would rather never see another bookshop again by now?

Carry on to Walmgate Bar, the only one with a barbican left. If you wish, follow the walls back to Nunnery Lane Car Park . . . eventually. If you have more time why not go to hire a cycle at nearby 16 Lawrence Street (tel. 26664), *York Cycleworks & Cycle Hire*? Three speeds £2 a day; ten speeds(?) £2.50 per day. If you have brought your own bike why not leave it to be serviced? Special accessories, spares, books, etc., available. York is the place to cycle—it is flat enough.

Shops in York are normally open between 9.00 a.m. and 5.30 p.m. and the half-day closing is Wednesday. Happy shopping!

MULBERRY HALL

# More famous buildings

HERE is a York Alphabet of famous buildings. It does not include churches, which are dealt with elsewhere, nor famous buildings already mentioned in other parts of the guide. Many buildings are easily reached from the wall walk.

**Art Gallery,** Exhibition Square (tel. 23839)

Look in the entrance archway to find four impressions of York artists: Etty (painting), Flaxman (sculpture), Carr (architecture) and Camidge (music). Go inside to find an old master for there is an excellent collection of European paintings dating from 1350 to 1800. See if you can find later works by Etty, Whistler, Sickert and Paul Nash. There are some interesting paintings showing York as it was a hundred and more years ago. Guided tours can be arranged. Contact the Curator. Catalogues, prints and postcards are available at the sales counter. There are special exhibitions from time to time.

*Opening times:* Monday–Saturday 10.00 a.m. to 5.00 p.m. Sunday 2.30 p.m. to 5.00 p.m.

*Admission free* most of the year but in season 20p from June 2nd.

**Assembly Rooms,** Blake Street (tel. 59881, ext. 342)

When York was the centre for great balls, parties and assemblies in the North during the 1700's this was where most of the action occurred. The central hall with its 52 columns, polished floor and chandeliers is magnificent. Built between 1732 and 1736 by the Earl of Burlington it is similar to London's Mansion House. Look for a mural showing Emperor Constantine entering York.

*Opening times:* Monday–Friday 10.00 a.m. to 4.00 p.m. (June 1st to August 31st) except when in use. Closed Saturday and Sunday.

*Admission free.*

Enquiries to the Estates Department, 5 St. Leonard's Place (tel. 59881, ext. 342).


**Black Swan Inn,** Peasholme Green (tel. 25236)

Perhaps the oldest inn in York but originally, in the fifteenth century, the home of a rich merchant. General Wolfe, when a child, lived in the house. He was later to defeat the French at Quebec, the world's quickest battle—it was over in ten minutes with Wolfe the victor, but dead. An upstairs room was used for cockfighting when the house became an inn later.

*Open to adults* during normal licensing hours.


**Guildhall,** St. Helen's Square (tel. 59881)

Behind the Mansion House and facing onto the river. The first Guildhall was built in the fifteenth century as a meeting place for the guilds but it was destroyed by fire during an air raid in 1942. The present building is a fine restoration opened by the Queen Mother in 1960. Look for the stained-glass window showing the history of York; the bosses in the roof; the coat-of-arms; gifts from Münster and New York; secret doorways and the underground passage called Commonhall Lane. This marks where the river was forded by the Romans and also their main road. Council Meetings

65

are held about every four weeks. The public can attend.
*Opening times:* Monday–Thursday 9.00 a.m. to 5.00 p.m.
Friday 9.00 a.m. to 4.30 p.m. Saturday 10.00 a.m.
to 5.00 p.m. May–October only. Sunday 2.00 p.m. to
5.00 p.m. May–October only.
*Admission free.* Ring the bell on the counter for attendant
to take you to the Inner Room, Council Chamber
and Commonhall Lane.


**King's Manor,** Exhibition Square (tel. 59861)

Read the plaque outside first. Then look at the coat-
of-arms above the doorway. Is the 'N' backwards? Can
you see the CR which stands for Charles Rex—who was
he? You will know by now that this building was once
the Abbot of St. Mary's house. When the abbey was
destroyed by order of Henry VIII it became the HQ
of the Council of the North. Did Henry VIII and
Catherine Howard once stay here? James I did and
you can see his initials at the foot of the front doorways.
Now the house is part of the University of York.

*Opening times:* Courtyards only open to the public.
Report first to the Porter's Office. Open all year
10.00 a.m. to 5.00 p.m. daily.
*Admission free.*


**Mansion House,** St. Helen's Square (tel. 59881,
ext. 222)

York was the first English city to build an official
home for its Lord Mayor. It is more than ten years
older than London's Mansion House. There are superb
rooms and York's insignia, regalia and civic plate are
kept there. These are things like the Sword of State, the
Great Mace, the Lord Mayor's Chain, punch bowls,
salvers, etc.

*Not open* though visits may be made by prior arrangement with the Lord Mayor's Personal Assistant, c/o
The Guildhall.

66

*The entrance to Gray's Court, Chapter House Street.*

**Merchant Adventurers' Hall,** Fossgate (tel. 54818)
The Hall belonged to York's most important and richest Guild. The building dates from 1357. Look for the Guild's coat-of-arms and banners, the undercroft where pensioners lived, the Pancake Bell and the chapel windows. The little garden by the Foss is very pleasant.
*Opening times:* April–October weekdays 10.00 a.m. to
4.30 p.m. November–March 10.00 a.m. to 4.00 p.m.
*Admission charge.*


**Merchant Taylors' Hall,** Aldwark (tel. 55452)
Built by a medieval guild of tailors. Brick outside conceals a hall of 1400 inside with fine timber features, especially the roof. There is a huge fireplace. The building was restored in 1969. Nearby the site of St. Helen-on-the-Wall's church has been excavated. Examination of skeletons from the burial ground has given much information about the diseases of the people of medieval York.
*Opening times:* May–September weekdays 10.00 a.m. to
4.00 p.m. Other times by arrangement only.
*Admission free.*


**Minster Library,** Dean's Park (tel. 25308)
This is the place to see Guy Fawkes baptism details also many other ancient books and manuscripts. Once, the Library was the chapel of the Archbishop's Palace which stood in the shadow of the Minster.
*Opening times:* Monday–Friday 9.00 a.m. to 5.00 p.m.
*Admission free.*


**St. Anthony's Hall,** Peasholme Green (tel. 59861, ext. 274)
Built in the fifteenth century for the Guild of St. Anthony. Later became a poorhouse, house of correction, a school and now the Borthwick Institute of Historical Research. There is a pretty garden here.

*Opening times:* Monday–Friday 9.30 a.m. to 1.00 p.m.
2.00 p.m. to 5.00 p.m.
*Admission free.* Main hall open. Any enquiries to the
Secretary.


**St. William's College,** College Street (tel. 24426)
Close to the Minster. Built in 1453 as college for
priests. Later used by Charles I as Royal Mint and for
his printing press. Has some very fine timbered roofs.
Look for the many carved figures, especially St. William.
Nice courtyard and a restaurant. Brass rubbing centre
open daily 10.00 a.m. to 6.00 p.m. Sundays 12.30 p.m.
to 6.00 p.m. Admission free.
*Opening times:* Monday–Saturday 10.00 a.m. to
5.00 p.m.
*Admission charge* to the upper floor.


**Theatre Royal,** St. Leonard's (Box office tel. 23568)
Dates from about 1740 when the entrance was in
Duncombe Place. It was one of the most famous
theatres in the country. It has had several different
fronts to it and one of them was taken to Fulford Road
and partly re-built there. The Foyer and restaurant
were added in 1967. The dressing rooms are in a cellar,
once the undercroft of St. Leonard's Hospital. Look for
the figures of Shakespeare and some characters from his
plays towards the rooftop at the front of the Theatre.
Plays, ballet, musicals, pantomime, etc. Coffee Bar,
Theatre Bars, Theatre Club, Exhibitions, Young
People's Theatre Company (contact Chris Wallis
tel. 58162). Put yourself on the mailing list free.
Backstage visits can be arranged by contacting the
Public Relations Officer.


**Treasurer's House,** National Trust, Behind the
Minster (tel. 24247)
Stands on the site of Roman buildings. You can see a

69

*The oak-beamed medieval hall of the Guild of Merchant Adventurers.*

Roman pillar base in a cellar also some medieval masonry but the house is mainly seventeenth century and later. Until 1547 the Treasurers of the Minster lived here. Inside the furniture, fireplaces and ceilings are very good. The garden is lovely and there are the best views of the Minster. Can you find the gravestones of a dog and parrot in a corner? John Goodricke saw stars from this house (see *Famous People*). Have a look in Gray's Courtyard nearby, reached from Chapter House Street.

*Opening times:* April–October daily 10.30 a.m. to 6.00 p.m. November–March closed.

*Admission charge:* Party rates for 15 and more but not on Sundays or Bank Holiday Mondays. Apply to the Administrator.

### Twelfth Century House, Stonegate

Down a narrow passage off Stonegate at No. 52A. Part of a Norman house, one of the oldest houses in York.

*Opening times:* Daily 9.00 a.m. to 10.00 p.m. (October–March 6.00 p.m.).

*Admission free.*

### University of York

Take a No. 5 or 19 bus to Heslington, two miles from the city centre for a walk around one of Britain's newest universities, opened in 1963. There is a fine lake with many attractive buildings and Heslington Hall a rebuilt Elizabethan mansion. Visitors can also arrive by car and park on the campus. Normally the public cannot go into university buildings but there are frequent events held in Central Hall and Lyons Concert Hall which can be attended (details from Tourist Information Centre, De Grey Building, back in the city).

# Sweets in York

DO you fancy a Polo, Smartie, Aero or Kit Kat? If so, you have come to the right place for York is the centre of the sweet-making industry. Terry's, Rowntree's and Craven's are the three big sweet firms which began as small shops in the city but then, in the nineteenth century, expanded so much that they needed to build large new factories on the outskirts.

Not only have the firms built pleasant factories in well-planned surroundings but they have introduced many improvements to help their workers and also the city. For example, Rowntree's built a model garden village at New Earswick, a few miles north of York, in 1902, especially for their workers. It is still being extended and is well worth a visit.

Now these firms have been merged with other well-known groups, for example, Terry's with Colgate Palmolive and Rowntree's with Mackintosh's but they still produce their well-known brands and many more besides. Here is a quick guide to when your favourite sweets were introduced:—

1881  Rowntree's Fruit Pastilles
1890  Mackintosh's Celebrated Toffee—the first toffee
1893  Rowntree's Fruit Gums
1912  Chocolate first made
1917  Chocolate coated toffee
1923  Rowntree's Table Jellies
1933  Black Magic
1935  Kit Kat and Aero
1936  Quality Street and Dairy Box
1937  Smarties and Polo
1948  Polo Mints
1957  Week-End and Munchies
1959  Caramac
1960  Good News

1962  After Eight
1963  Toffee Crisp and Tootie Frooties
1965  Jellytots
1976  Yorkie

York is the centre of a sweet empire because Rowntree-Mackintosh have factories in Norwich, Halifax, Castleford, Edinburgh, Newcastle, Hadfield, Glasgow, Leicester, in France, Germany, Holland, Australia, Canada, Ireland and South Africa. The sweets, of course, are exported all over the world to places as far apart as Abu Dhabi and Aruba, Zambia and Zaire.

Factory visits by school parties and others are rarely possible but information can be obtained from the Public Relations Officer, Rowntree-Mackintosh, York YO1 1XY (tel. 53071); J. Terry & Sons Ltd., Bishopthorpe Road, York (tel. 26261); M. A. Craven & Son Ltd., Candyland, York YO2 6BA (tel. 792121).

# Famous people

WHICH Roman emperors died in York? Who made York capital of half of Britain? What is the link between York and Constantinople? Did King Arthur drive the Saxons out of York? Who was Erik Bloodaxe? Did a York man kill Macbeth? Who was pressed to death by a door? Who really did ride from London to York on a horse? Which deaf and dumb man saw the star Algol for the first time? Who is Dr. Slop? Who is the Railway King? Why is York linked to 'a town like Alice'?

York, like other great cities, has its famous men and women. Often they are record breakers because they were either the first to achieve something or they were well-known throughout Britain and the world for a special contribution. Sometimes, it was for a bad thing, like Guy Fawkes; sometimes for a good life, like St. Margaret of York. Let's look at the famous people of York from the dawn of time to the present day.

## Emperors

As we have seen, the Roman Ninth Legion set up its headquarters at York in A.D. 71 and it soon became the most important centre in the North. Just over fifty years later *Emperor Hadrian* arrived to plan the famous Hadrian's Wall which stretched across England from the River Tyne to the Solway. It was a defence and a frontier against the wild Picts and Scots. It took about fourteen years to build and today you can walk along it to relive the past.

Roman emperors came and went but two never left. *Emperor Septimus Severus* divided Britain in two and made York capital of the northern half. He made it the home of his Imperial Court for the last three years of his life, dying there in 211. A century later *Emperor Constantius* died in York in the year 306. Legend says that his son,

74

*Constantine the Great,* was born in York in 274 and that his mother Helen may have been British. Later she became St. Helen and today there is a church called St. Helen in St. Helen's Square. Constantine was the only Roman Emperor to be proclaimed in Britain and he became Emperor of a united Empire covering most of Europe with its centre at Constantinople, named after Constantine himself. He was the first Christian Roman Emperor and made Christianity the official religion. So it is possible to say that a York man gave his name to Constantinople!

## Kings and Rulers

*King Arthur* turns up in most places and so it is not too surprising that he is supposed to have driven the Saxons from the city and to have protected St. Samson as the Archbishop. There is a redundant church of St. Samson's in Church Street to this day. Another story tells of the last king of York, Peredur, being killed in battle in the year 580. Was this *Sir Percival* of the Knights of the Round Table? Some people think so.

*King Edwin of Northumbria* was baptised a Christian on Easter Day, 627, by *Paulinus* who later became first Bishop of York. He was really the first in the long line of Archbishops of York, the present one being the ninety-third. On the site of the baptism a small wooden church was built—the first York Minster.

When the Vikings captured York in 866 they were led by *Ivar the Boneless.* Many Viking kings ruled later but little is known about them. *Erik Bloodaxe* was the last pure Viking ruler of York and it says so on the T-shirt you can buy from the York Archaeological Trust and on the mug where his fierce bearded face says 'Erik Bloodaxe Rules OK'. His reign was short.

Then York was ruled by Anglo-Scandinavian earls under Danish law. The greatest was *Siward* who defended the North against the Scots and invaded Scotland, killing King Macbeth in battle in 1054.

Siward is believed to have lived in a palace near St. Olave's Church which he founded and in which later he was buried.

*King Harold,* who was killed at the Battle of Hastings in 1066, came to York only three weeks before his death. He passed through the town on the way to Stamford Bridge where he met and defeated a Norwegian army. His successor, *William the Conqueror,* came several times to York to squash rebellions in the 1060's and he built two castles to hold the town. When he had the *Domesday Book* compiled in 1086 it contained a good description of York at that time.

*Richard II* wanted to make York his capital and he bestowed many privileges on it. One was a Sword of State, another was to make York a county in its own right. When he died in 1399 many citizens led by Archbishop Scrope revolted against the new king. Scrope was executed outside the city walls and his tomb can be seen in the Minster. Look for Richard's badge of the chained hart in the Minster.

*Richard III* also was fond of York and his son was invested as Prince of Wales in the Minster but died shortly after in 1484. Richard himself was killed at the Battle of Bosworth in 1485, the last of the Plantagenets. The citizens sent an army to help him but it arrived too late. You can see a scroll commemorating Richard in the Minster Chapter House.

So you can see that many of the kings mentioned were unlucky, often coming to a 'sticky end'. *Charles I* was the same. He made York his temporary capital in 1642. He set up his Court at King's Manor, the Royal Mint nearby and his official printing press in St. William's College, near the Minster. The Roundheads began the Siege of York in 1644 but soon, after the defeat at the Battle of Marston Moor, the city fell. Not long afterwards, in 1649, Charles was beheaded in London, the only English king to be executed by his people.

## Scholars and Saints

*Alcuin* was born in York in 735. He was a great teacher. He was educated at the Minster School, which became famous throughout Europe. St. Peter's School, Clifton, claims direct descent from this school founded in 627. If this is so then it is one of the oldest schools in Britain. Alcuin left York to become adviser to Emperor Charlemagne and had a great influence on the civilisation of the areas now known as France, Belgium and Germany. His name is remembered by Alcuin College, built in 1967 as part of the University of York.

*St. William of York* was once simple William Fitzherbert, nephew of King Stephen. He became Archbishop of York in 1153 and, as he entered the town in triumph Ouse Bridge collapsed with the crowds on it. William prayed that none might drown and none did. Although he did not seem such a holy man, when he died a year later many people thought he should become a saint. He did so in 1226 and his tomb in the Minster became a centre of pilgrimage. Find the St. William window in the Minster which shows some of his miracles, including the collapsing bridge. St. William's College, near the Minster is also a reminder of this little-known man.

*Miles Coverdale*, who was born in 1488, is one of the greatest sons of York, but he is often wrongly forgotten. He produced the first complete English Bible in 1535 and the official Great Bible of 1539. Many church services including the psalms sung today, are following Coverdale's versions. Like Alcuin, he had a great influence throughout Europe.

*St. Margaret of York* was a butcher's wife who hid Catholic priests in her house to save them from torture. Although this was not proved, she had a door placed across her body piled with stones until she was dead. Because she died for her faith she was made a saint in 1970. Margaret Clitherow's House, No. 35 the

Shambles, is now a chapel and it can be visited daily except when in use for services. Recent research, however, seems to show that Margaret's house was *actually* on the other side of the street!

### Rebels and Highwaymen

*Guy Fawkes* was born in a house in Petergate or Stonegate in 1570. He was baptized in St. Michael-le-Belfry church nearby and you can see the Register in the Minster Library open at the page showing this. He was a pupil at St. Peter's School. He became a devout Catholic and plotted to blow up the Houses of Parliament. He was captured and executed in 1606. Everyone else burns a guy on November 5th, but not St. Peter's. They don't like to burn past pupils!

*Sir Thomas Fairfax* was a local landowner who became a Roundhead general during the Civil War and fought against King Charles. He was at the Siege of York in 1644 when he stopped his troops looting and damaging the city. He fought at the battles of Marston Moor and Naseby. He approved the trial of the King but was against his execution.

*John William Nevison* was a highwayman also known as 'Swift Nicks' who was hanged in York in 1685. He made the famous ride from London to York, *not Dick Turpin* otherwise known as John Palmer. Dick was born in Essex, convicted of horse stealing at York Castle and hanged at the Knavesmire or York Tyburn in 1739. You can see his tombstone in St. George's Churchyard, George Street. The cell he occupied can be seen in York Castle Museum. He remains a legend and went to his death on the scaffold bravely. In fact, he was the most notorious criminal of his time . . . and there never was a Black Bess! By the way, you could be hanged for horse stealing in those days but there was also plenty of evidence to show that Dick Turpin was a highwayman and murderer too.

78

## Reaching for the Stars

*John Goodricke* was born in 1764 and was deaf and dumb. He lived in the Treasurer's House in the grounds of the Minster. You can read a plaque to his memory there today. Not only was he interested in astronomy but he made a discovery which gave him an important place in the history of astronomy. He discovered 'variable stars' by observing Algol. When only 21 years old he was awarded a Fellowship of the Royal Society for his work but he died only a year later. Now one of the colleges of the University of York is named after him.

*Thomas Cooke* was born a few miles away from York in 1807. He was fascinated by Captain Cook's travels and began to teach himself astronomy and navigation. In 1837 he set up in business at 50 Stonegate making telescopes. His work became well-known and he moved to larger premises in Coney Street, then to a factory on Bishophill called the Buckingham Works. He began to make surveying instruments, steam engines and turret clocks and other astronomical instruments. Just before he died he was working on the largest telescope in the world which was completed in 1870, two years after his death. His sons carried on the business and it is now part of Vickers Instruments Ltd. producing equipment to analyse samples of moon rock brought back by astronauts. Thomas Cooke made outstanding contributions to the manufacture of telescopes and other instruments but one of the most charming of his constructions is the Little Admiral Clock in Coney Street.

## Writers and Artists

*Laurence Sterne* was a novelist and vicar born in 1713. His best known works are *Tristram Shandy*, first published in York, and *Sentimental Journey*. His uncle, Jacques Sterne was Precentor of the Minster and lived in the Treasurer's House. Laurence lived in Shandy Hall, Coxwold, which is now open as a museum.

Dr. Slop was a character from *Tristram Shandy* based on *Dr. John Burton* who helped to found the first county hospital in York in 1740. There is a memorial to him in Holy Trinity Church, Micklegate.

Other famous writers, poets and actresses include *Lindley Murray* who was an American but came to retire in York in 1784. He produced an English Grammar which was a standard work for years. He is buried in the Friends' Burial Ground, Bishophill. *Neville Shute* author of *A Town Like Alice* and *On the Beach* came from York. So did the poet *W. H. Auden* who died in 1973 and *Judi Dench*, well-known actress of stage, film and TV. Don't forget that according to Daniel Defoe *Robinson Crusoe* was also born in York in the year 1632!

One of York's most famous artists is *William Etty* born in 1787 well-known for his figure paintings. You can see his statue outside the Art Gallery in Exhibition Square. Inside there is a room devoted to his work. There is a memorial to him in St. Olave's, Marygate, where he is buried. Besides being a painter William did a great deal to save the Walls of York from being destroyed by the Corporation in the 1820's.

**The Railway King**

*George Hudson* was born in 1800 near York. For years he was a draper in the city; then he was left £30,000 by an uncle. With this he began to invest in railways, soon becoming a millionaire and also Lord Mayor of York three times. He did more than anyone to make York a railway centre, which it still is to this day. His greatest day was 29th May, 1839, when the York & North Midland Railway opened to immense celebrations. He established many other railways and encouraged the growth of seaside resorts but, in 1849, he fell from power and died a fairly poor man in 1871. He is buried at Scrayingham, a few miles north east of York. George Hudson Street, not far from the Railway Station, is a reminder of the Railway King.

*George Hudson, the 'Railway King'.*
*(Photograph courtesy of the National Railway Museum, York)*

## Architects

The designers, builders and masons of York in earlier times may never fully be known but they achieved a miracle we can see today. Later architects such as *John Carr* and the *Atkinson family* were famous in 18th-century York producing buildings such as the Assize Courts and many fine houses. *Joseph Hansom* was born at 114 Micklegate in 1803. Though he was an architect he is better known as the inventor of the Hansom Cab.

## Sweets and Famous Men

The *Rowntree* family and the *Terry* family became famous during the 19th century for making sweets. Each firm grew from small beginnings until now they are one of the main industries of York. Rowntree concentrated on cocoa and chocolate. *Joseph Rowntree* is also remembered for creating a 'model village' for the workers at New Earswick and *Seebohm Rowntree* for three surveys into poverty in York (see the section on *Sweets in York*).

So the roll of honour could go on . . . *William Tuke*, a Quaker like the Rowntrees, founded the first modern mental hospital in 1796 known as the Retreat. *George Russell*, who died in 1951, expert producer of lupin flowers in more than sixty colours. *Dr. John Kirk* whose great collection of bygones led to the foundation of the largest and most popular folk museum in Britain, the Castle Museum, York. As George V once said 'The history of York is the history of England'.

# Fixing a tour

YOU can guess that York is likely to be a spooky place but you need to know where to find the ghosts. Luckily, an expert on haunted York will lead you on a two-hour walking tour to visit some of the sites even if he cannot guarantee that a ghost will actually appear. (See also *Ghosts of an Ancient City*, by J. V. Mitchell (Cerialis Press, York, £1.95.)

Tours of ghostly and historic sites are organised by *Enrichment Travel*, 7a St. Sampson's Square (tel. 52232) Monday to Friday from Spring Bank Holiday to the end of September. You have to meet in the Oak Room at the Black Swan Inn, Peasholme Green at 8.00 p.m. No advanced booking is necessary, just turn up. The latest prices are adults £1.00 and children 50p. Groups can arrange tours all through the year on request if they give at least 24 hours' notice.

There are several other Tour Organisers such as the *Association of Voluntary Guides* based at the De Grey Rooms, Exhibition Square (tel. 21756). They offer free conducted two-hour walking tours of the city starting from Exhibition Square at 10.15 a.m. and 2.15 p.m. daily, from Good Friday to the end of October. Additionally, there are walks starting at 7.15 p.m. daily in June, July and August. The route includes the Multangular Tower, St. Mary's Abbey ruins, a wall walk from Bootham to Monk Bar, Goodramgate, Holy Trinity, and the Shambles. Special interest walks are also provided including Roman York; Riverside York; Stained Glass; Georgian York; Alleys and Lanes; City Walls; Medieval Churches, during summer months. There are tours of floodlit York in September and October. Conducted tours can also be arranged in advance for groups and individuals throughout the year, but not for school parties or walks in the suburbs.

*Gateways*, c/o Mrs. N. Hearing, 15 Poppleton Road, York, YO2 4TT (tel. 793335) specialise in tours of York particularly for school children. The popular tour is the Minster, part of the city walls, St. Mary's Abbey, Museum Gardens, Stonegate and the Shambles which takes about two and a half hours. Irrespective of time however, the charge is still 25p per child and bookings can also be made for any of the Museums through Gateway. They will do tours for your own chosen route too. All tours available all year round.

If you are a fan of Richard III you can follow the landmarks showing his links with the city by joining a tour of Richardian York starting from the Library Square, Museum Street, every Sunday in season at 2.30 p.m. This is organised by the *Richard III Society York Branch*.

*Yorktour*, Baxby Manor, Husthwaite (tel. 03476 572) also offer guided tours of York and the area around. If you have your pen-friends or foreign visitors with you this is the tour to do as they are multi-lingual.

You can arrange conducted tours of *York Minster* through the Information Officer, St. William's College, College Street, York (tel. 24426).

Coach tours of the city start from the Railway Station and last about one and a half hours. They operate several times a day between April and October inclusive but as times may be variable check with the Tourist Office. The 1980 prices were adults £1.10, children 55p. Tours of the area round York are also operated by local firms such as Pullman Coaches (tel. York 22992). See *A Day Out From York*.

Of course, it is also possible to arrange conducted tours by car through *Yorktours* and *Badger Tours*, 19 Brompton Road, Clifton (tel. 705874) both in the city and country but they are expensive.

For *Horse Drawn Danish Carriage trips* round the city in summer, contact Mr. B. W. Calam (tel. 769490).

84

# Railway mania

YORK is one of Britain's busiest railway centres. It has one of the longest platforms and its beautiful, curving, eight-hundred-foot-long train shed is like a railway cathedral. The first railway museum in Britain was opened in York in 1928 but the New National Railway Museum, which is another reason for York being the Mecca of railway enthusiasts, opened in 1975.

It was the first national museum to be sited outside London and is officially a branch of the Science Museum, London. Built in an old steam engine shed, it has two original turntables and a direct rail link to the main line. This helps when locomotives and carriages need to be moved.

Where can you see a statue of George Stephenson? Where is the oldest vehicle preserved in Britain that runs on a track? The first iron railway bridge in the world? Queen Victoria's favourite railway train? The oldest surviving British travelling post office coach? The oldest vehicle with flanged wheels? The last British Rail cattle trucks? The last steam locomotive to be built by British Rail? Where can you see a Banana Van and a horse in a Dandy Cart? Why in the National Railway Museum, of course, and many more things besides such as the record breaking *Mallard* world speed record holder for steam locomotives at 126 m.p.h.

But there are far more items in store which are exhibited from time to time as the displays are changed. Normally, there are some 25 locomotives and 20 items of rolling stock on the turntables for you to see including Royal Coaches, a full-sized express cut in half to show its inside and the experimental version of the Advanced Passenger Train.

*A Special Exhibitions Gallery* and the *Balcony* contain

more displays on the history of British railways. There are railway toys, models (of trains and ships), posters, signs, railway tickets, etc., etc. A model railway gallery will open in 1981 to include classic 'toy' models of early tin plate examples as well as electric models and fine scale (7 mm) models to form the basis of a detailed working model layout of the museum. *The Front Gallery* has early uniforms, paintings, photographs, stained glass station windows, restaurant car and other items.

*The Lecture Theatre* seats up to eighty and, although it is mainly intended for school parties the public can attend. Film shows for the public are often part of the holiday activities presented by the museum. There is a *Refreshment Room* serving light meals (with interesting views over the Main Hall and outside). *The Museum Shop* is near the entrance and sells souvenirs, publications, etc. An essential buy is *The National Railway Museum Guide*, an excellent and colourful booklet. Don't forget to look at the exhibits outside the Museum.

For information about visits by special parties contact The Education Service, National Railway Museum, Leeman Road, York YO2 4XJ (tel. 0904 21261). You must book at least three weeks before the intended visit on the official Booking Form. You will also receive a very useful guide to the educational facilities and *Planning your visit to the National Railway Museum*. This gives ideas for interesting things to do on your visit. Free services include assistance in the galleries, talks, films, lectures, use of a study coach and a refreshment coach. School and organisational visits are best made in the off-season. Avoid June, July and August.

The National Railway Museum is very handy if you arrive by rail as it is behind the Main Railway Station, down Leeman Road. However, because of low bridge limits along Leeman Road only single deck coaches can reach the Museum. Car parking is available from one

*From the National Railway Museum: (top) rolling stock, and (bottom) a sectioned ex S.R. Merchant Navy Class, Ellerman Line loco. (Photograph courtesy of the National Railway Museum)*

87

hour before opening to 6.00 p.m. but there is a charge. Still, considering that the admission to this unique museum is free, that seems reasonable.

Your family can join the Friends of the National Railway Museum which helps in all possible ways. It organises meetings, festivals, open days, competitions and hopes to develop the model side as well as restore *Mallard* to running order. Contact the Secretary, c/o National Railway Museum.

*Opening times:* Monday–Saturday 10.00 a.m. to 6.00 p.m. Sunday 2.30 p.m. to 6.00 p.m. Closed New Year's Day, Good Friday, May Day, Christmas Eve, Christmas Day, Boxing Day. Watch the press for details of special events.

*Admission free* during normal opening hours.


**Visits to York Station**

Party visits are possible every day between 9.00 a.m. and 2.00 p.m. Obtain an application form from the Area Manager, British Rail Eastern Region, West Offices, York YO1 1HT (tel. 0904 53022). Normally party size has to be not less than 12 and not more than 20 persons. The minimum age limit is 12 years and individuals between 12 and 17 must be accompanied by an adult. One adult to a party of 12–15 persons and two adults to a party of 16–20. Small groups of up to 6 in number (with an adult) can sometimes be attached to other parties visiting. For all visits applications in writing must be made at least four weeks before intended visit. The current charge for a visit for a party of between 12 and 20 persons to one depot is £10 plus £1.50 V.A.T. For a person or persons attached to a party for which arrangements have already been made the charge is £1 each plus 15p V.A.T. If your party arrives by rail and you can show a valid ticket plus the permit obtained in advance the visit is free.

*Trainspotters* are allowed onto the platforms providing

they possess a valid ticket. However, this may not be possible when traffic is heavy.

There is a *Railway Mania Bar* in the Station Hotel for adults in your family.

There are numerous railway societies including the York Branch of the North Yorkshire Moors Railway Society (first Tuesday September–April, Centenary Chapel, St. Saviourgate); Railway & Canal Historical Society (monthly at Railway Institute); Society of Model Engineers (monthly, Outdoor Railway, Moor Lane, Dringhouses. Public running of railway first Sunday, May–September); York Model Railway Society (Tuesday, Friday 7.30 p.m. at Railway Institute, minimum age 14); York 'O' Group (Tuesday and Friday 7.30 p.m., 49 Vine Street—models 7 mm/ft. 1930's trains). For further details of such societies contact Central Library, Museum Street, York YO1 2DS (tel. 0904 54144).

# Eating out

YORKSHIRE is famous for its food which you can buy from the many lovely shops in York or taste in some of the cafes and restaurants. Have you ever tried Yorkshire Pudding with gravy, on its own? Tripe and Onions? Black Pudding? Fish and Chips cooked in beef dripping? Woof Pie? Filey Coble Stew? Wright's Pork Pies? York Ham? Brontë Biscuits? Yorkshire Parkin? Curd Cheesecake? Wilfra Apple Cake from Ripon? Wensleydale Cheese and Applepie? Yorkshire Teacakes? Why not start now whilst you are in York, at least some of them should be available.

There are some good stories told in a book called *A Taste of Yorkshire* by Theodora Fitzgibbon (Pan Books) with many recipes which you could try at home too.

**Picnics**

You may wish to buy food from shops and, in fine summer weather, take this on a picnic. If so, there are some pleasant places in the city where you can eat your food. *Museum Gardens* is a lovely setting and also very handy for the city centre. If you want to be near the river you can go to *Riverside Gardens* near Lendal Bridge and sit facing the fine Guildhall. Further downstream, near Skeldergate Bridge you have *St. George's Gardens* which are always open. They are opposite the Castle Museum and Clifford's Tower. *Memorial Gardens*, Leeman Road, are quite close to the Railway Station but they are out-of-the-way and quiet. *Dean's Park*, behind the Minster is also pleasant and quiet. Further off, either down Bishopthorpe Road or walking along the riverside, you reach *Rowntree Park*. Here you will find a boating lake, bowls, tennis, children's playground, an open air swimming pool, toilets, cafe, caravan and camping site.

90

**Take Away**

Here is your chance to get at the fish and chips. One of the handiest places if you are in the centre is Petergate Fisheries, 97 Low Petergate, also Gillygate Fisheries; Gladstone's Corner House, King's Square, and Neptunes, 93 Micklegate.

But you could try a take-away kebab from Spartan Kebab House, 10 North Street. You can have take-away vegetarian snacks from York Wholefood, 98 Micklegate or stay in the restaurant which is open every day except Sunday for lunches. Tea and coffee are served between 10.00 a.m. to 12 noon and 2.00 to 4.30 p.m. Greensleeves Natural Foods, 108 Fishergate also specialise in wholefood dishes some of which can be taken away. Stanleys, 56 Goodramgate, have over 76 English and Chinese dishes to choose from in their restaurant which is open every day of the week including Sunday. Some dishes are part of the take-away service. Stanleys also cater for school parties. Don't forget to look for the hot-dog stall in St. Sampson's Square, you could find it quick and handy especially in the evenings. Maybe you will hear the hurdy-gurdy organ with its little monkey which is sometimes nearby. Oh, another thing, you might be interested in is that Greensleeves has live folk music on Thursday, Friday and Saturdays in a relaxed atmosphere with 10% discount for students. You can telephone your take-away orders on 54750.

**Departmental Stores**

You can get a good snack or meal at a fair price in several of the big departmental stores and they usually serve children's portions. Leak & Thorp, Coney Street, provide quick snacks in the Toastrack and, if you have more time and money you can have homemade English dishes in the Norseman Restaurant together with a view of the River Ouse. Debenhams, also in Coney Street, has a coffee bar, York Cooperative in

George Hudson Street has a buffet grill where hot meals and snacks are available. There are also facilities at Marshalls, Davygate, and W. P. Brown also in Davygate. Boyes Riverview Cafeteria has opened recently and is handy for the Walkway along the River Ouse.

Don't forget that you can buy meals and snacks in places already mentioned such as the National Railway Museum and the Theatre Royal. Here the Salad Bowl Restaurant and the Coffee Shop are particularly pleasant.

**Favourites**

Are you looking for haggis and chips? If so go straight to McDowells, 10 Coppergate, or if you prefer (and can afford) steak with the haggis go to the Railway King Hotel, George Hudson Street. Perhaps you could manage a Danish Open Sandwich? If so, try the Danish Kitchen, 12 High Ousegate, where in addition you can have pastries and fresh cream cakes.

For USA style 100% hamburgers where better than Dreamville, King's Square. This popular spot has 36 flavours of real dairy ice cream! And you can have sparklers on the ice cream! Romano's, 27 Goodramgate, has an ice cream parlour serving delicious ice cream in many varieties and is open daily including Sundays. They are happy to serve pizzas and toasted sandwiches for children and families.

Homemade steak and kidney pies and fruit pies from Charlie Brown's 68 Gillygate and splendid chilli con carne from Lew's Place, King's Staith both offering children's portions. More homemade cakes, bread, etc., from Fanny's, 24 Pavement and Riverside, 15 Low Ousegate.

If you want a medieval setting in a courtyard then St. William's College, College Street, is the place for you. Salads, quiches, soups, homemade scones and cakes in a handy place for the Minster and very popular with the kids, especially as they can do Brass Rubbing here.

The Baked Potato Wagon at 33 Swinegate has over

twenty different homemade fillings to choose from in your splendid take-away baked potato and they are open seven days a week. Why not pay them a visit?

Perhaps you would like to try Filey Coble Stew and have a river view at the same time. Then the Viking Hotel, North Street, is the place if you can afford the experience.

The Priory Street Sports and Community Centre, Micklegate, has a cafeteria run by Ann and Derek (tel. 39968) with pine tables, benches and a relaxed atmosphere for families. Half portions served. Birthday parties can be arranged here with the nearby gym available for high jinks by 3 to 8 year olds, particularly where noise can be tolerated and no cleaning up afterwards. Menu planned with parents. After-panto parties also catered for.

Cooplands, Davygate, have self-service and specialise in homemade steak pies, pasties, etc., with children's portions and room for 120 people.

As for coffee bars you have a vast choice but if you would like an old-fashioned, vintage place, try the Kiosk Coffee Bar in Stonegate. Shop downstairs and tea, coffee, snacks served upstairs in clean, pleasant surroundings. Good loos. If you like the coffee or tea you have just drunk you can buy a packet downstairs in the shop.

Now, if by any chance you have missed your breakfast, try the Olympia Coffee House, St. Sampson's Square, open daily including Sundays 8.00 a.m.–7.00 p.m.

For a *Daily Mirror Good Grub Guide* recommendation the name of the place is The Breadbasket, 30 Goodramgate, where families are especially welcomed and the speciality is value for money.

Of course, these are only a few of the many eating places in York. A full list is available from the Tourist Office, De Grey Rooms, where an *Accommodation Guide* can also be obtained. *The Access Guide for the Disabled* (see *For Handicapped Children*) has a full list of cafes and restaurants and how accessible for wheelchairs, etc.

# Day out from York

YORK is so centrally placed that it is possible to reach a great variety of countryside and seaside in a short time. Even Leeds and the urban areas of West Yorkshire are only about thirty miles away. But remember that you have to come back as well as go out and so it's best to limit yourselves to places within, say, forty or fifty miles of York.

## A Dash to the Sea

One of the best coastlines in Britain stretches from Bridlington, near Flamborough Head, to the River Tees in the north. You can reach *Bridlington* easily in an hour by car. Here there are excellent sands, a picturesque harbour, boating and fishing, sailing, the Old Town with its splendid Priory Church, amusements, playgrounds and Sewerby Hall with all its attractions. See the *Dalesman Miniguide Bridlington*.

*Filey and Scarborough* are a little further north but still only about forty miles from York. Again both have many fine attractions and there is a Butlin's Camp near Filey which can be visited by day tourists. Scarborough has its impressive ruined castle on a headland separating two sandy bays. There is Marineland with famous performing dolphins and each September the Cricket Festival. See the *Dalesman Miniguide Scarborough*.

*Whitby*, together with *Robin Hood's Bay* and *Staithes* provide the smuggler's coastline. Steep slopes lead down to the sea. There are caves and rock ledges, fossils galore! Visit St. Hilda's famous Abbey, stand below Captain Cook's statue or near the arch made from a whale's jawbone at Whitby. Go to Pannett Park Museum for the story of this great whaling port. Buy some of the famous jet and look at the Frank Sutcliffe collection of photographs of old Whitby. If you obtain a Captain Cook Trail leaflet from the Tourist Office in

Whitby you will be able to track down some of his old haunts but you will need a car and time for this as it goes across the Moors.

## The Sporting Life

*Cricket:* Scarborough Festival, early September. All the great players and the touring team. A really traditional event. You can visit a Test Match or Yorkshire games at Headingley, Leeds, only 28 miles away from York.

*Fishing:* sea fishing along the coast in places mentioned. See *Along the River* for coarse fishing nearer York.

*Soccer:* nearest first division side is Leeds United at Elland Road (tel. 716037).

*Gliding:* Ouse Gliding Club at Rufforth Aerodrome four miles from York (tel. Rufforth 320), flying on Saturdays and Sundays. Yorkshire Gliding Club fly from Sutton Bank, twenty-two miles from York (tel. Sutton 237). Visitors are welcomed at both clubs and can take flights. There is a five-day holiday course at Sutton Bank weekly from May–September.

*Golf:* there are over sixty courses within an hour's drive from York. Visitors welcomed with club hire at many. Near York there are courses at Fulford, Strensall, Heworth and Pike Hills. Near Leeds many more. See *York Miniguide.*

*Rugger:* League games at Clarence Street Stadium, York (tel. 24252) and Castleford (26 miles), Leeds (Headingley also). Rugby Union at Clifton Park, Shipton Road, York (tel. 23602).

*Sailing:* again at the seaside, also see *Along the River* section.

*Motor Racing:* speed hill climbs five times each summer and spring at Harewood (Stockton Farm, 20 miles) and Castle Howard (15 miles) in April and October.

*Motorcycle Racing:* annual national and international road race meetings held at Oliver's Mount, Scarborough.

*Swimming:* good facilities at York but remember also the excellent beaches at the seaside . . . only the sea breezes can stop you.

*Walking:* especially the famous Pennine Way, the Lyke Wake Walk (do it to be entitled to wear the coffin badge), the Cleveland Way, the Wolds Way.

## National Parks

Two of Britain's largest and most beautiful National Parks are within easy striking distance of York. The Yorkshire Dales Park has trails through woodland and moorland with the limestone scenery being highlighted on the Malham Tarn Trail. Contact the National Park Information Officer at Yorebridge House, Bainbridge, North Yorkshire DL8 3BP (tel. 444), for more details.

The North York Moors National Park has spectacular scenery and some of the largest forests in Britain. There are information centres at Danby Lodge, Sutton Bank and Pickering Station. At this station you can catch the North York Moors Steam Railway for a trip across the moors to Goathland and Grosmont. Daily service from April to November. Gala Days in May and September (tel. Pickering (0751) 72508/73535). Contact National Park Information Officer at The Old Vicarage, Helmsley, North Yorkshire YO6 5BP (tel. 657), for more details about Park nature and forest trails, etc.

## In Search of History

There are castles, cathedrals, abbeys and churches galore around York. Here are just a few of the very special ones: Beverley Minster (30 miles)—a rival to York. Has its own Saint. The town is really interesting too. Byland Abbey, Rievaulx Abbey and Helmsley Castle are all fairly close to each other and you can visit them on one trip. They are about 25 miles from York. You will see really lovely ruins in a fine setting. Scarborough Castle has already been mentioned and it is certainly outstanding, so too Whitby Abbey.

Twenty-four miles north of York there is Ripon Cathedral, quite small but dating from A.D. 655. Each night at 9.00 p.m. the Wakeman sounds his curfew horn and St. Wilfrid rides through the streets on the first Saturday in August.

Whilst you are in this area (or better still on your visit to Sutton Bank) call into the Kilburn workshops of Thompson's the famous carvers of the Mouse Trademark which you remember seeing in York Minster and many other well-known buildings. Visitors are very welcome.

A few miles away from Ripon is Studley Royal Country Park and Fountains Abbey. Lovely for a whole day out for a picnic. Deer Park open all year. Abbey and Gardens daily November 1st–March 31st 9.30 a.m. to 4.30 p.m. Sundays 2.00 to 4.30 p.m. Rest of year 9.30 a.m. to 5.30 p.m. (May, September 7.30 p.m.; June, July, August 9.30 p.m.). *Admission charge.*

As for great and small houses there is no shortage at all. Perhaps the most famous is Castle Howard (15 miles) which is really a palace. There is a costume museum and the Great Yorkshire Steam Fair is held here every August. Burnby Hall Gardens (11 miles) has the finest collection of water lilies in Europe and there are interesting relics from all over the world in the House. Visit the home of the famous Brontë sisters at The Parsonage, Haworth (47 miles in the opposite direction). You will then begin to realise what *Wuthering Heights* is all about, at least the bleak moorland setting. The house is very much as though the sisters have just gone out and will return very soon.

Look in the *York Official Guide* for details of the many more castles, abbeys, houses, churches and gardens to visit.

## Zoos and Things

How could you miss *Flamingo Land Zoo*? Especially if you are on the way to Scarborough for a day out. It is 25 miles from York and there is so much to see and do that it would need all day just there. More than 1,000 animals in nearly natural surroundings, a lake with real flamingos, a fun fair, a jungle cruise, a model railway centre, gnomeland, a children's farm, an adventure playground, a pottery workshop, a miniature Flying Scotsman to travel on . . . who could ask for anything more? Plenty of space for picnics, meals and snacks if you wish. There is a Holiday Village attached where you can stay. Special events take place regularly in season and visits of stars like Red Rum and Jimmy Tarbuck.

*Opening times:* From the first Sunday in March to the end of October. 10.00 a.m. closing at various times according to the time of year. Located off the A169 Malton–Pickering road at Kirby Misperton (tel. 065 386 287).

*Admission charge:* Children under three free. Party rates for coach parties over twenty in number.

*Mother Shipton's Cave and the Dropping Well.* A sort of witch lived in the cave. She forecast the future, often very accurately. Now there is a museum here. The unique spring water can turn objects to stone when they are dipped in it. Go to Knaresborough (19 miles).

*Opening times:* Daily from 10.00 a.m. to 5.00 p.m. (April–October inclusive).

*Admission charge.* Refreshments and parking available.

*Hornsea Pottery.* A long way to go (43 miles) but very worthwhile especially as you can have a day by the sea and also visit Yorkshire's largest lake, Hornsea Mere.

Hornsea Pottery is famous the world over for its fine wares. Here you can go on a factory visit, see the mini zoo, the model village, the country crafts and gift shop (with pottery seconds), use the play area and picnic park, have rides on the bus . . . in fact you can have a day to remember and it's all **FREE**, See *Dalesman Miniguide Hornsea.*

*Opening times:* 10.00 a.m. to 5.00 p.m. every day, extended to 6.00 p.m. during July, August and all Bank Holidays. Closed for one week at Christmas. Parties book in advance (tel. 040 122 161). Small charge for Factory Tour.

*Lightwater Valley Country Park* is just off the A6108 Ripon–Masham road and provides a super day out for the family. There is a mile long railway, boat rides, an adventure playground, a nine-hole golf course, covered golf driving range, putting greens, archery range, three restaurants, shops, crafts, cross-country rides on 'go anywhere' vehicles, mini motorbike rides, fifty acres of self-pick fruit, a modern piggery where you can sometimes see piglets being born. About 25 miles from York.

*Opening times:* April–May weekends only plus Bank Holidays and Easter Tuesday, 10.30 a.m. to dusk. End May–end August 10.30 a.m. to 7.00 p.m. daily. September weekends only 11.00 a.m. to 6.00 p.m. October Sundays only 11.30 a.m. to dusk. Last entrance one hour prior to closing.

*Admission charge.* (Tel. 0765 85321/85213.)

Many of these trips are easiest by car but if you enquire at British Rail, York Station (tel. 25671) for services and excursions you may find some useful. Also, buy the *York Bus & Coach Planner* (5p. from the Tourist Department, De Grey Rooms) for full details of services. Details of excursions from York Pullman Bus Co., Bootham Tower, ·Exhibition Square (tel. 22992), also West Yorkshire, Rougier Street (tel. 24161) for tourist tickets, York Country Roamer Tour, Castle Howard, etc.

# Read all about it

MANY useful books and addresses have been mentioned already but here is a handy list of essential information which you can turn to when you are in a hurry:—

*York Tourist Information Centre*, De Grey Rooms, Exhibition Square, York YO1 2HB (tel. 21756/7).
*Opening times:* Mid-May to end of September, Monday to Saturday, 9.00 a.m. to 8.00 p.m. Sundays 2.00 p.m. to 5.00 p.m. Early October to mid-May, Monday to Saturday, 9.00 a.m. to 5.00 p.m.

You can obtain the *York Official Guide and Miniguide* (50p) which has a street map, parking details, book lists about York including educational materials and much more on what to see in the city. Also *What's On: a fresh weekly guide for visitors and residents*; *York: Where to Stay* and very many more publications. Posters and leaflets in the Centre will give you even more up-to-date information.

*Central Library, Museum Street* (tel. 54144) has a marvellous local history room and also details about various city activities. Apply here for details about societies, the Sports Directory, Living in York, and Access for the Disabled.

*Yorkshire & Humberside Tourist Board*, 312 Tadcaster Road, York YO2 2HF (tel. 707961) will send you further information about the region.

*York & District Education Centre*, College of Ripon & York St. John, Lord Mayor's Walk (tel. 28225) has sheets and booklets on various buildings, etc., produced by local teachers. Lists obtainable from the Secretary.

*North Yorkshire County Guide* (25p) a mine of information especially about the region. From the Public Relations Officer, County Hall, Northallerton, North Yorkshire DL7 8AD (tel. Northallerton 3123).

Newspapers are the most up-to-date source of events so you should keep your eye on the *Yorkshire Evening Press*, 15 Coney Street (tel. 53051) which comes out Monday to Saturday with a Pink Sports on Saturday. The *Yorkshire Gazette & Herald* comes out weekly on Thursdays. Look for the special holiday supplements which the papers bring out from time to time. The *Yorkshire Post* and the *Evening Post* are published in Leeds but they have a great deal on York and its area.

There are several local newspapers produced by voluntary groups such as the *York Free Press*, 73 Walmgate, *Flag* and *Tom-Tom*.

*Citizens Advice Bureau*, at York Community Council House, 10 Priory Street (tel. 52524).

*General Post Office*, 22 Lendal (tel. 28901).

*Opening times:* Monday–Friday 9.00 a.m. to 5.30 p.m. Saturday 9.00 a.m. to 12.30 p.m.

*Police Headquarters*, Fulford Road (tel. 31321).

*Casualty Hospital*, York District Hospital, Wigginton Road (tel. 31313).

*Taxis.* ABC Taxis (tel. 59693), Fleetways (tel: 53344/24998), Streamline (tel. 38833/23737).

*Markets* daily except Mondays at Newgate Market, near the Shambles.

Because so many school parties visit York we thought it would be a good idea to reprint information from the York School Visits Advisory Service and a special letter from the North Yorkshire Police which both contain useful information and valuable advice for all young people in York. We are grateful for permission to reprint the material overleaf.

## SCHOOL VISITS ADVISORY SERVICE
### Tourist Information Centre, Exhibition Square, York
### Tel. 21756/7

The School Visits Advisory Service, working in close liaison with several other organisations, offers practical assistance and guidance to visiting school parties. Although we are unable to supply literature in quantity, we have a large selection of different items available. We can suggest itineraries for your visit, be it a half-day or of several days duration; parking places for your coach; explain the intricacies of our one-way traffic system; tell you where to obtain a reasonably priced meal or suggest a picnic spot. We will provide you with a free list of York literature, or perhaps you would prefer to buy our fully illustrated Official Guide (include Mini Guide and Map) for 50p, plus 26p postage. The Mini Guide and Map is also available separately, price 10p, plus 10p postage.

We are willing to try to help all who write or telephone us, but we regret that we are unable to assist individual pupils with their topic work.

Please write again explaining your particular interest in York.

### Educational visits to York—general advice

1. Winter visits will be more beneficial to your party. Come between October and March if possible. At certain times during the summer it is impossible to visit some places of interest without prior arrangement.

2. Include some of the lesser known, but equally important, places of interest in your itinerary. All visitors see the Minster and the Castle and Railway Museums, but miss places like the Art Gallery, Impressions Gallery of Photography, Merchant Adventurers' Hall, Merchant Taylors' Hall, St. Mary's Abbey, Treasurer's House, Yorkshire Museum and the York Story (St. Mary's Heritage Centre), which tells the story of York in sound and vision.

3. You should aim for a teacher/pupil ratio of 1:10.

4. Most places of interest are situated within the City Walls, which a small area—it would be helpful if you could divide your parties into small groups,

102

visiting different places at different times.

5. Lost children. At the request of the local police, we suggest to organisers of parties of children visiting the City that each child should be provided with a label showing name and address, school or organisation, registration number of coach and place and time of departure.

6. In your preliminary planning you may find it useful to see what local teachers have produced. Call at the York and District Education Centre, College of Ripon and York St. John, Lord Mayor's Walk, York, where examples of worksheets, etc., may be purchased. Please note that postal enquiries or bulk orders of literature cannot be dealt with outside the area of North Yorkshire and North Humberside. Subjects covered by the worksheets include: the walls and bars of York, medieval crafts in York, St. Mary's Abbey, visiting Georgian York, and many others. A resources list is available from the Centre.

7. Literature available from the School Visits Advisory Service.

## Free

*BTA illustrated leaflet.* (Brief historical notes on places to see.)

*Places of Interest.* (Opening times, party rates of admission.)

*Restaurants willing to accept school parties.* (Seating capacities and prices.)

*Educational resources for visitors.* (List of useful addresses.)

*Index Street Plan.* (Location of places of interest.)

*Information Sheet.* (Details of tours, brass rubbing centres, river trips, etc.)

*Accommodation List*

*The Arms of York*

*Famous people connected with York*

*Roman York*

*Anglo-Viking York*

*Medieval York*

*Tudor and Stuart York*

*Georgian York*

*Victorian York*

*York in the 20th Century*

103

*Fortifications of York*
*Medieval Guilds of York*
*Trade and Industry in York*
*York Communications*
*Hospitals and Almhouses in York*
*Education in York*
*Reading List*
*Events List* (weekly)

## On Sale

| | |
|---|---|
| *Official Guide* (including *Mini Guide*) | 50p + 26p postage |
| *Mini Guide* | 10p + 10p postage |
| *Roman York* | £1.00 |
| *Short Guide to the Roman Fortress at York* | 25p |
| *Bars and Walls of York* | 50p |
| *Georgian Houses in York* | 30p |
| *Georgian Public Buildings in York* | 30p |
| *Civic Plate and Insignia of York* | 25p |
| *York Walks* (4 itineraries with questionnaire) | 15p |
| *Minster Walks* | 15p |
| *Castle Museum Walks* | 15p |
| *Brush with History at York* (Painting Book) | 30p |
| *Brush with Steam at York* (Painting Book) | 30p |
| *National Railway Museum Workshop* | 30p |
| *St. Mary's Heritage Centre* (York Story) | 20p |
| *York Mystery Plays* | 40p |
| *City of York and the Minster* | 60p |
| *Castle Museum Handbook* | 40p |
| Castle Museum Pamphlets | |
|    *Sir Thomas Fairfax* (Soldier and Scholar) | 15p |
|    *John Carr* (Architect) | 15p |
|    *Thomas Cooke* (Telescope Maker) | 15p |
|    *George Harland* (Countryman) | 15p |
| *York in Colour Filmstrip* | £3.25 |
| "*We called them Tingalaries*" cassette | £2.60 |
| Slides. Six different sets at 90p each | 90p |
| *Stonework in York*   Tour 1 Minster | 1p |
|       Tour 2 General | 1p |
|       Tour 3 Walls | 1p |
| *Woodwork in York*  Tour 1 | 2p |
|       Tour 2 | 1p |

| | |
|---|---|
| *York Churches* | 1p |
| *York Pubs* | 2p |
| *Curiosities of York* | 2p |
| *Guildhall* | 1p |
| *Assembly Rooms* | 2p |
| *Common lanes and alleyways of Medieval York* | 2p |
| *York's surrounding countryside* | 3p |

To:—

## TEACHERS, AND OTHERS, RESPONSIBLE FOR GROUPS OF YOUNG PEOPLE VISITING YORK

The York Division of the North Yorkshire Police welcome you to the City of York. Should you feel in need of assistance or directions,· please do not hesitate to contact any Policeman or Traffic Warden or to telephone the Police Office.

Approximately 2¾ million visitors come to the City of York annually and you can visualise that this causes problems, one of which arises when large parties of children move together through busy, narrow and unfamiliar streets. Many of you will have made excellent arrangements for your party's visit and we apologise if you feel that these reminders are unnecessary. Unfortunately, our experience over the years has been that some do not plan with sufficient care to avoid possible disruption and distress.

### Programme

Each member of the party should have in his or her possession a document which clearly gives the following information:—

   (a)   Name of School
   (b)   Places to be visited and time of arrival at each
   (c)   Name of Coach Company
   (d)   Coach Park used—complete on arrival, if necessary
   (e)   Time of bus or train departure.

### Traffic

The streets of York are narrow, the traffic is heavy and waiting cars cause congestion, especially in the centre of the City. This is aggravated where children are allowed to walk through the streets or cross the roads in one continuous file.

Please split your party into small groups with adequate supervision of each group.

## Supervision

It is well known that children allowed to visit premises, shops, and so on, unescorted by a responsible person, may get into mischief. In the past, some children have been granted free time whilst in the City and this has resulted in some stealing from the multiple stores and larger shops. When this happens, distress is inevitably suffered by the children immediately concerned, and inconvenience and delay may be caused to the remainder of the group. It is suggested that, at all times, children should remain in the charge of an adult in the ratio of at least one adult to ten children.

It is sincerely hoped that you enjoy your visit to the City of York and that you will return.

With best wishes.

*This letter is issued by the North Yorkshire Police under the auspices of the York Crime Prevention Panel.*

# For handicapped children

YORK is not the easiest of places for handicapped people. The walls and many public buildings have steps and awkward approaches; footpaths are narrow and winding; streets are busy and congested; there are narrow alleys, kerbs and other obstacles around. Shops, restaurants, theatres, cinemas, parks, bus stations, hotels may unknowingly provide difficulties. It is important to find out about access for the handicapped.

Luckily, work by Fulford Comprehensive School pupils and their teacher, Mrs. C. Kellett, resulted in an excellent *Access Guide to York for the Disabled* which contains detailed information about door width, counter height, step height, parking, inside steps, wheelchair access, etc. This applies to transport, hotels, entertainments, churches, toilets, public houses and restaurants, shops and social centres. Copies can be obtained from Mrs. C. Kellett, Fulford School, Fulfordgate, Heslington Lane, York.

The Guide is particularly useful for visitors to the city as it details access to the Art Gallery, Castle Museum, Guildhall, Heritage Centre, Merchant Adventurers' Hall, Merchant Taylors' Hall, Museum Gardens, National Railway Museum, St. William's College, the Treasurer's House and the Shambles.

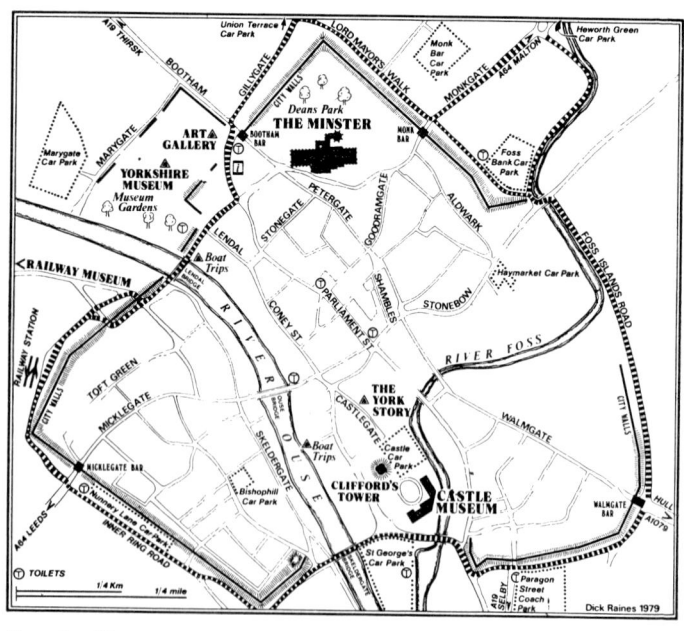

*Reproduced by courtesy of the Castle Museum.*

108

# Index

111

112